Britain and Ireland in
Early Christian Times

LIBRARY OF MEDIEVAL CIVILIZATION

EDITED BY

PROFESSOR DAVID TALBOT RICE

CHARLES THOMAS

Britain and Ireland in Early Christian Times

AD 400–800

THAMES AND HUDSON · LONDON

Printed in Great Britain by Jarrold and Sons Ltd, Norwich

ISBN 0 500 56002 1 clothbound
ISBN 0 500 57002 7 paperbound

Contents

Preface

7

Introduction

11

1 The End of Roman Britain

13

The Legions Depart
Sub-Roman Times
The Native Principalities
A Host of Tongues

2 Invaders and Colonists

31

Hengist and Horsa
Excursus: Arthur and Mount Badon
Painted Men in the North
The First Scots
Irishmen in Mann and Wales
The Far South-West
To Armorica and Beyond

3 Christianity

71

The Church in Roman Britain
Bishops and Dioceses
Ninian and Patrick
The First Monasteries
St Augustine at Canterbury
Northumbria's Golden Age
The Christian Dead

4 Home and Hearth   112
   Fortress and Citadel
   The Lesser Dwellings
   Farmers and Stockbreeders
   Men of Special Gifts
   Warriors and Mercenaries

Select Bibliography   136

List of Illustrations   140

Index   143

Preface

In a large volume entitled *The Dark Ages* which was published in 1965, an attempt was made to survey the cultural heritage to which Europe was to succeed when once the Middle Ages dawned around the year 1000. The publishers have now decided to issue some of the chapters that appeared in that volume, rewritten and in extended form, as small, modestly priced, but well-illustrated, monographs bringing them up-to-date with recent studies. The first to appear was David Wilson's *The Vikings and their Origins*; the second is the book to which these words form the introduction. It is entitled *Britain and Ireland in Early Christian Times: AD 400–800* and covers developments throughout the British Isles, including Ireland; special stress is laid on the Celtic areas, primarily because up to now less has been written about them than about the Anglo-Saxon ones.

That the first two studies to be published deal with Britain is to some extent fortuitous. Both chapters, however, aroused particular interest when they appeared in *The Dark Ages*: both deal with our homeland and both to a great extent cover mainly uncharted ground, unlike the surveys devoted to the Byzantine world and to the Carolingian and Ottonian epochs; here an attempt was made to place these highly developed phases in a context of growing European culture, whereas the chapters on the Vikings, on Britain, and others that dealt with the Merovingian or Visigothic cultures were more exploratory.

Again, the period between about 300 and 800 in Britain is fascinating in itself. Just as the study of ruins has a strange, nostalgic fascination, so also does the story of the decline of Roman power and the gradual disappearance of the benefits that it had brought, both material and spiritual. Over all the northerly part of this once great empire, the lights of civilization were being extinguished, from the shores of the Black Sea to the Atlantic seaboard of Britain; only in the Mediterranean area, in the territory immediately subservient to Constantinople, the new Rome, did ordered control and stable life persist. Elsewhere the once imposing administrative buildings, the luxurious country houses, the strong fortresses and defensive structures were left deserted and barren, at best to be used by uncivilized squatters. New waves of immigrants were arriving, each in turn bringing further, more intensified destruction, wreaking greater devastation to older glories. But it was not wholly an age of decline. Rather one should look on this phase as the crucible in which a whole series of new, even if immature, ideas were distilled. And towards the end of the seventh century the unifying power of Christianity was able to exercise a strong stabilizing influence and to lay the foundations on which a new culture could develop. The new culture was to flourish with especial vigour in Northumbria, outpacing any similar movements on the continent of Europe anyhow till Charlemagne arrived on the scene. It is to this progressive phase that Professor Thomas' book forms the introduction.

In treating of this period there has been a tendency in the past either to concentrate on archaeological minutiae or to stress the highlights, like the treasure of Sutton Hoo, the sculptures of the Northumbrian crosses, or the glories of the so-called Hiberno-Saxon school of miniature painting. A refusal to follow either of these trends characterizes Professor Thomas' approach. He has concentrated on the central narrative, without deviating in favour of the spectacular or the better known. At first glance the story seems to be terribly intricate and confused. For the ordered, centralized system of the Roman age there was substituted a disconnected, interrupted progression of small groups, which continually warred with one another or infiltrated one another's territory. Conquest, trade, missionary activity, a search for new worlds and even, one suspects, a desire of exploration for its own sake, were the governing factors; confusing linguistic and cultural admixtures were the result, so that the economic and historical developments that ensued are hard for the specialist to define, harder still for the uninitiated to follow. Thirty, even twenty, years ago the former task would have been well-nigh impossible; now, thanks to the painstaking archaeological, linguistic and historical research of numerous scholars, it has become possible to attempt the task. It is a pioneering one, and Professor Thomas would himself be the first to admit that it is still far from complete. But he has for many years made this age the centre of his very special study in the field and at his desk alike and, thanks to his guidance, we can now advance along routes which form a very essential basis for the understanding of future developments in Britain. His book is a basic one, which cannot fail to interest all who are concerned with the subsequent history of the whole of Britain.

DAVID TALBOT RICE

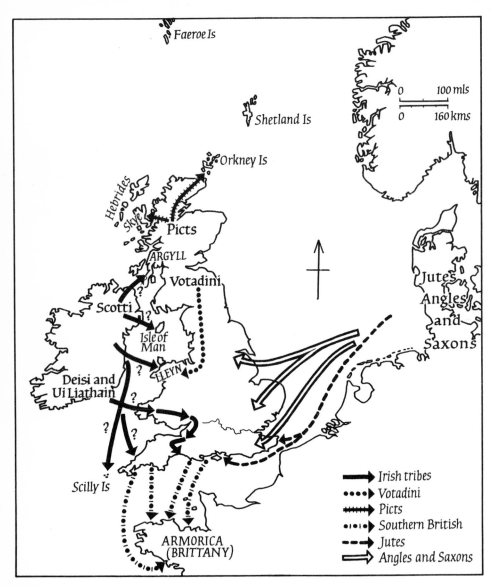

Faeroe Is

Shetland Is

Orkney Is

Hebrides

Skye

Picts

ARGYLL

Votadini

Scotti

Isle of
Man

LLEYN

Deisi and
Ui Liathain

Scilly Is

ARMORICA
(BRITTANY)

Jutes,

Angles
and
Saxons

0   100 mls

0   160 kms

→ Irish tribes
••••▶ Votadini
+++++▶ Picts
•ı•ı•▶ Southern British
- - ▶ Jutes
⇒ Angles and Saxons

1   The former Roman province of Britain was invaded or colonized from the east, by various Germanic peoples; from the north, by Picts and scarcely Romanized north British; and from the west, by numerous Irish tribal groups. Unsettled conditions in the fifth century, and fear of the Irish, rather than Anglo-Saxon assaults, may have prompted the British migrations to Armorica (now Brittany). Other minor movements shown here would include Pictish expansion westwards to Skye and the Outer Isles, and northwards to Orkney and Shetland; inter-dynastic conflict in Ireland; and scarcely definable movements within the remains of Roman Britain

Introduction

In the four centuries between the end of the Roman occupation of Britain and the first Viking raids, much of the pattern of both medieval and modern Britain was laid down. The full story of those centuries – and they are centuries where the normal sources of historical information, if not lost, are dark indeed – is not yet written. I do not presume to offer more than a personal view, a most imperfect and compressed one, of the period. It rests on studies, other people's rather than my own, in which it is not always easy to say just where archaeology stops and history begins.

R. G. Collingwood once wrote: 'As works of imagination, the historian's work and the novelist's do not differ. Where they *do* differ is that the historian's picture is meant to be true.' Truth, in Collingwood's sense, can surely be no more than the reflection of what the writer believes to have happened – perhaps, within that definition, no more than those happenings which he deems to have had important and subsequent influences. To me, three things above all characterize these centuries. They are the migrations and settlements (which were by no means *1* confined to those of the Anglo-Saxons), the rise of Christianity, and the diversity of spoken and written languages. Seen against these broad factors, the usual problems of detailed brooch typology, of precise shapes of spearheads or helmets, and of whether or not the Saxons first broke in the valley bottoms with heavy ploughs, lose much of their cogency. At the risk of being accused of undue selectivity, even of superficiality, I have tried to present a general picture with those three factors always in mind. The reader who is drawn to the Bibliography (p. 136) will find a most carefully chosen range of writings, which should lead him on to bigger and better pictures. An acquaintance with the course of events in Britain and Ireland at this stage, and it is one that hardly any school or university textbook seems to offer, is not only rewarding in itself; it is, I have long been convinced, fundamental to any grasp of later developments in our history, language, arts, and socio-political structure right through the Middle Ages and up to the present century.

There is a deliberate bias in this book towards the north and west of Britain; not because the Anglo-Saxon world is any less interesting or less important, but because early English aspects have already been covered in a number of excellent studies. The pre-Norman history and archaeology of most areas outside lowland England is far less accessible, especially in a compressed or digestible form. It should be made clear that 'Britain' means the modern England, Wales, Scotland, Mann, and all the offshore groups of islands: 'Ireland' is geographical Ireland, not just the present-day Republic. The adjectives 'British' and 'Irish' refer to these respective and physically distinct units; 'Insular' is just a convenient way of writing 'British and Irish'.

My debt to a large circle of friends and fellow students will be apparent, in the text as well as in the illustrations. Too numerous to acknowledge individually, they will perhaps accept collectively my gratitude. In curtailing the story at AD 800 – for the chapter which this book replaces in the parent volume, *The Dark Ages*, went up to AD 1066 – I would direct the reader to David Wilson's companion study, *The Vikings and their Origins*. This continues the British and Irish story from the late eighth century onwards, from an appropriately fresh angle.

A. C. T.

Chapter One

The End of Roman Britain

There is no single year in which we can claim, with confidence, that the Roman occupation of Britain ended – suddenly, definitely, and for ever. In T. S. Eliot's words, the end was marked, not with a bang, but a whimper. The process now appears to have covered a good half-century, and the selection of some such horizon as AD 400 (or 410, or 425) to mark off Late Roman from sub-Roman times is an aspect of convenience rather than of reality.

The Legions Depart

In 406, the Roman army in Britain, obliged to watch from these remote side-lines the apparent collapse of the Empire under massive barbarian onslaughts, elected usurpers of its own. The choice eventually settled upon Constantine ('Constantine III') in 407. In Italy, the Goths had already forced the Imperial court, under the official emperor, Honorius, to withdraw from Milan to Ravenna. Various Germanic tribes who had crossed the Rhine at the end of 406 were threatening the whole of northern Gaul. Constantine crossed with his troops to the Continent and secured the Rhine frontier, possibly with certain privy arrangements. Basing himself further south, at Arles (where, in 411, he was to be captured and slain at the bidding of Honorius), he succeeded in adding Spain to his short-lived dominion.

2 Constantine (known as 'Constantine III'), emperor AD 407–411; gold *solidus* with portrait head

This was not the first occasion on which Roman Britain – this term implies the present England and most of Wales – had been deprived of its official garrison and of its supreme commander. In 383, when Gratian was

3 The usurper Magnus Maximus, proclaimed in Britain in AD 383; a gold *solidus*, mint of Trier

4 Ivory diptych panel, 32·2 cm high, showing the general Stilicho, regent in Britain from AD 393. Son of a barbarian (probably Vandal) cavalry officer, Stilicho's heroic stature is mentioned by contemporary writers; here he is shown in conventional military pose *c*. 395

Emperor of the West, a Spaniard, Magnus Maximus, was 'made emperor in Britain through the treachery of the soldiers', as a fifth-century Gaulish chronicle records. Maximus, long remembered in British tradition as *Macsen*, overcame Gaul and Spain, taking most of the army from Britain for this purpose, before his own downfall in 388.

Between these two episodes, and after the reign of Honorius' father, Theodosius (379–95), certain measures to re-establish the defences of Britain had been taken. These are to be associated with a powerful general, Stilicho, in the period from 395 to 400. They, and the significance of the adventures of Constantine III and of Magnus Maximus, have to be appreciated in the light of the corresponding dangers. Roman Britain was organized in four provinces, to which a fifth, Valentia, was added some time in the 370s. For the purposes of civil administration, Britain was a diocese, one of a dozen within the Empire, and was subordinate to a praetorian prefect of Gaul residing at the great city of Trier. It was in every sense an outpost of empire, the limit of the civilized world, with its northern frontier marked by Hadrian's Wall; but in 343, and more especially in 367–69, confidence

5 Hadrian's Wall, completed by about AD 127; the northern frontier of the Province of Britain, here seen looking eastwards near Housesteads

4

5

6 Saxon Shore forts in Britain:
   1 Brancaster (*Branodunum*)
   2 Burgh (*Garionnonum*)
   3 Bradwell (*Othona*)
   4 Reculver (*Regulbium*)
   5 Richborough (*Rutupiae*)
   6 Dover (*Dubris*)
   7 Lympne (*Lemanis*)
   8 Pevensey (*Anderida*)
   9 Portchester (*Portus Adurni*)

in the efficacy of this barrier against the untamed
Picts, Caledonians, Attecotti, and other wild barbarians,
must have been irretrievably fractured. Again, the
hundreds of miles of coastline constituted a secondary,
and far less defensible, frontier. On the western flank,
Britain within and without the frontier, from Argyll to
Cornwall, lay open to the Irish, whose currachs could
ferry slave-raiders and booty-hunters over numerous
short sea-crossings. Eastwards, most of lowland England's
flat coast and shingle beaches were exposed, not only to
the vessels of the Picts, but to those of the northerners
from Europe – peoples of Scandinavia, of Frisia, and of
Germany beyond the Rhine. All these could and did
repeatedly plunge their bloodied hands into the treasuries
of Britannia. Schemes of defence in the late fourth century
had to contemplate not only the long land frontier in the
6–8 north, but a network of coastal signal-stations, shore-
forts, camouflaged patrols, and naval bases housing what
amounted to a home fleet.

What is now clear is that, after 407, 'the defence of
Britain' against the barbarians (acting alone or in concert)
meant something very different from that implied in the
provisions of the third, or even the fourth, centuries.

7, 8 Forts of the Saxon Shore. *Above*, Portchester (? *Portus Adurni*), at the north end of Portsmouth harbour; the eastern water-gate, from the interior. *Below*, Burgh Castle (*Gariannonum*), with the river Waveney in the background, near the Suffolk coast. Both were in use in post-Roman times. Burgh Castle, Bede's *Cnobheresburg*, was given just before AD 640 by king Sigeberht of the East Angles to the Irish monk, Fursa, for a monastery

There are allusions which have been construed to mean that the official pattern of military command continued, in the expectation that Britain would as soon as feasible be regarrisoned; even that it *was* so reoccupied, at least in part, in the late 420s. It has been argued that certain major posts – Count of the Saxon Shore, and the command of some kind of field-army – were still in effective being; and that a 'Count of Britain' operated under Imperial rescript after 417, if only in south-east England. We cannot yet be clear as to all this. What may be suspected is that, militarily, Britain was falling apart like an abandoned and scattered jigsaw puzzle. Concepts of linear defence had perforce given way to ideas of defence in clumps, the scattered efforts of urbanized communities based on surviving walled towns – what Wheeler has called 'the domestic trainbands of the individual cities'. That the actual effectiveness of these groups was as much in the hands of non-British settled mercenaries as in those of the native Romanized Britons must also be considered. At the same time, in the west and in the north – over half, if not more, of the former Roman diocese – both power and society were reverting to a condition, that of native principalities, reminiscent in certain respects of the pre-Roman Iron Age four hundred years before; having, moreover, to accommodate within that framework entire communities of Irish origin, to whom the stability and tradition afforded by Roman bureaucracy were as cobwebs.

Sub-Roman Times

The fifth century AD continues to be the most obscure in our recorded history. Literary sources are external, or derived with difficulty from writings of later periods, and within a crude frame based on a few fixed points we cannot fully employ the relevant archaeological clues (of which, almost certainly, we already possess more than we can realize). For Britain about 400, our picture is mainly a literary one; for Britain in the decades after 500, another picture, partly literary, partly archaeological, is being constructed. The contrast between the two implies changes at every level of activity. It poses questions to which only contentious or stop-gap answers can be given, and those in no more than very general terms.

The expression 'sub-Roman' is a useful one, but it must be cautiously applied. It can legitimately refer to any area formerly within Romanized Britain. This excludes all of Ireland, Scotland north of the Antonine Wall (and possibly between the two Walls), and conceivably the less accessible and mountainous regions of Wales. The implication is that three and a half centuries of Roman influence, custom, and control took another century to run down, and this is demonstrable in many respects. A British variety of Vulgar Latin continued to be spoken; there were schools, men of learning, books. In certain settlements, the equivalents of town councils and some official positions still existed. Town life did not everywhere end – people were inhabiting, and for that matter building and rebuilding, certain towns as late as the middle of the century; and an increasing number of towns (London, York, Carlisle, Canterbury, Winchester) at last reveal hints of continuous occupation from Roman times to the present day. They must be added to others (Gloucester, St Albans, Silchester, Wroxeter – this is *9* also a growing list) where fifth-century occupation of some kind or other has already been shown. Coinage, in the guise of still-current Roman money of genuine Imperial origin, of dispersed fourth-century hoards of debased, clipped, overstruck, and even restruck obsolete *10* coins may (it has been seriously claimed) have circulated throughout the fifth century. There must, on the other hand, have been a steady economic rundown, caused by the loss of profitable military custom, by the disappearance

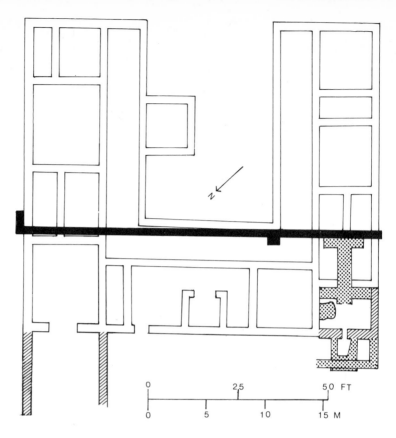

PERIOD 1 ... c. A.D. 370   PERIOD 2 ... LATE IV cent.

CORN-DRYING OVEN   PERIOD 3 ... EARLY V cent.

PERIOD 4 BUTTRESSED HALL ... V cent.

9 Verulamium (now St Alban's); ground plan, from 1960 excavations, showing a large town house of *c.* AD 370, with early fifth-century corn-drying oven, and foundations of a great buttressed hall (mid-fifth century?)

10 Part of Hoard II, Lydney, Glos, of 1,646 coins, deposited within a room of the bath building; fifth century. Most are tiny bronze *minimi* or *minimissimi*

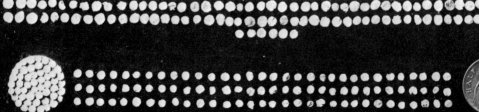

11 Bronze belt-buckle, 62 mm, from Crane Godrevy, Gwithian, west Cornwall. Of Roman inspiration, this is locally made and probably sub-Roman in date

of regular markets (and with this, the contraction of primary produce to a village or workshop level), by the difficulty of maintaining roads and rivers for wheeled and barge transport, and by the general insecurity surrounding the outlets for bulk products. This is surely reflected in at least three ways – the comparative scarcity of coinage (implying a reversion towards a barter basis), the disappearance of cheap mass-produced domestic pottery (which must be readily transported and swiftly distributed in bulk if it is to support any kind of industrial manufacture), and the evidence for the large-scale activities of individual craftsmen at this time (most notably in the fields of personal ornaments, weapons, and metal *11* vessels).

We can do little more than infer the general political history. Gildas (a British or Breton cleric writing in the decade 540–50) certain sources used in the period 720–30 by the Venerable Bede, lost chronicles or traditions enshrined in even later British writings, ideas which can be prised from contemporary Continental works, and inferences drawn (largely by analogy) from isolated historical suppositions, all suggest that – as one might guess – an internal power vacuum made itself felt by the second quarter of the century. Until, somewhat later, the external menace of the Germanic settlements relegated other matters to a position of secondary concern, the middle and late fifth century may have been a period characterized mostly by civil conflict and commotion. Given that, as communications faltered and as rural society withdrew into itself, matters of wider moment may have been irrelevant to large tracts of sub-Roman

Britain, we can make certain assumptions. We might infer that any conflict would tend to a polarization between a surviving 'Roman' party derived from continuing urban settlement in the south-east – this is perhaps the true sub-Roman world – and others, not necessarily prepared to renounce their status as *cives Romani*, who saw the immediate future in quite other terms. Such might have been those of regional domains, controlled in perpetuity by those in power and by their descendants, increasingly careless of whether walled towns survived or not and increasingly mindful of former British valour.

This interesting hypothesis can actually be argued (with variations according to taste) for the end of the fifth century. Had the Anglo-Saxon settlements never taken place, some major split in Britain as it then was might well have attained the status of reality in the sixth century. Essentially, by 410 or so, the apparatus of centralized Roman government and the parallel notion of a Council of Britain drawn from the leaders of the *civitates* (the major internal administrative divisions) broke down. John Morris, putting a very English viewpoint, summarizes what surely followed: 'The history of the next two centuries is the history of the failure of the British to replace that authority with a central government that could achieve permanent and general respect.' One might take this a stage further. The history of the next *four* centuries is the history of the reasons – in retrospect, their weight is all too apparent – which underlie that particular social and political failure.

The Native Principalities

Romanized Britain had itself been subdivided. London – Londinium, later Augusta – was the seat of the *vicarius*, the civil head of the diocese of Britain. There were the four *coloniae*, York, Lincoln, Gloucester, and Colchester,

12

12 Political map of Roman Britain showing approximate extent of the civitates, with principal towns or 'cantonal capitals', and major Roman settlements

the last three having territories of uncertain extent around the actual towns. The rest of England and Wales was parcelled out into the various *civitas* *civitates*. The word *civitas* possessed different meanings at different times in the Roman Empire, apart from its original sense of '(Roman) citizenship'; by the fourth century, we can regard its British context as one describing at once a sizable self-administrative and partly self-governing area, the (urban) seat of government allotted to that area, and the administrative and legal concept of the area and its seat as a distinct unit. Precisely which description really applied remains, as yet, a matter of scholarly argument, and without trying to translate *civitates* as 'cantons', we can take them as representing effective spatial divisions of Roman Britain and its inhabitants.

Civitates bore, for the most part, the names of the major tribes who occupied these areas at the time of the Roman conquest. Thus south-central Wales, home of the Silures, appears in an inscription as *Respublica Civitatis Silurum*. The *civitas* of the Belgae, a non-tribal creation covering Hampshire and parts of Wiltshire, Somerset, and a little of Gloucestershire, centred on Venta Belgarum (Winchester: the word *venta* means, possibly, a market-town). Save where obvious geographical boundaries, like the major rivers, can be applied, the exact division of Britain into *civitates* is not always clear; nor is it really certain how closely the divisions perpetuate prehistoric tribal territories.

The process whereby certain *civitates* during the fifth and the sixth centuries, evolved into independent principalities is historically irrecoverable. Our knowledge of this happening rests upon place-names, allusions in later historical sources, and what purport to be genealogies of the appropriate native dynasties preserved in some Lives of Saints and in medieval Welsh compilations. Cumulatively, they leave no room for doubt that this transition did occur, and occurred widely. *Civitates* in Britain may have originated in several ways; as in Gaul, certain tribes may have achieved this status through treaty relationships, others may have been at some stage what was called stipendiary *civitates*, and it is possible that some *civitates* were split and re-formed. We assume that the British were encouraged to select, and improve, one or other of their tribal centres to serve as the seat of government, and that by the late fourth century the normal pattern of government could be found. This involved a group of magistrates, supported by and elected through an *ordo* or council, made up of *decuriones*, the choice of whom was subject to rules of property qualifications, or inheritance, or otherwise limited. It was the local *ordo* that supplied delegates to any provincial council;

13 Late sixth-century tombstone, Cubert, Cornwall: '(The grave of) Conetocus, the son of Tegernomalus'

and magistrates and decurions alike, however Romanized, would in native terms tend to be drawn from the higher grades of hereditary landlordism, surviving from the pre-Roman Celtic system. St Patrick's father, Calpornius, was a Christian and happened to be a deacon, just as Patrick's grandfather Potitus happened to be a priest; but Calpornius, a fourth-century Briton in some north-western *civitas*, was also a decurion, owning a country estate with servants and maids, and this made Patrick (as he himself tells us) 'freeborn according to the flesh'.

In Iron Age times, Celtic-speaking society in Ireland and Britain exhibited a kingship surrounded by vestiges of much older attributes: ideas of the king's divinity, taboos surrounding his office, and the still-vital function as a war leader. Kingship was nevertheless not subject to direct dynastic succession. The succession, as Professor Binchy points out, was by kin-right, but as chaos would ensue without due control, certain practical limits (restriction of the kin-group, or nomination of a successor during life) were necessary. Whereas pre-Roman tribal monarchs (in Britain and Ireland as in Gaul) frequently bore names compounded with the word *rix*, 'king', their post-Roman counterparts are not so named. Certain sources refer to them as *tyranni* or tyrants, and the use of this word may have been influenced by a native term *tegernos* or *tigernos*, meaning approximately 'landlord' or *13* 'lord'. This last occurs in such personal names as that of Vortigern ('overlord'), a fifth-century ruler in some part of Wales who gained temporary predominance on a much larger scale. New titles appear, to meet new situations.

Very curious is the Welsh *brenin* ('king'), Cornish *brentyn* ('noble, sovereign'), which goes back to a British title *Brigantinos*: Binchy suggests that this, originally a name for the king of the northern tribe of the Brigantes, divine spouse of their national goddess Brigantia, was somehow transferred to western Britain by analogy. He writes: 'The new rulers were . . . "great kings" rather than tribal kings, and for them the old name of *rhi* [from earlier *rix*] was on longer appropriate.'

Who were these post-Roman figures? The interesting aspect of the native kingdoms at this time is not just that appropriate genealogies were duly supplied, as time went by; it is that the dynastic lists were taken back to suitable founders. That for Gwent, which replaced the *civitas* of the Silures in South Wales, early included a sub-Roman prince Caradauc – revival of a great name, Caratacus, son of Cunobelinus, long famous in British ears as that of the leader of a first-century anti-Roman revolt. Was descent implied, if not claimed? The list of kings of Dumnonia, a south-western British kingdom based on the *civitas* of that name, includes Eudav or 'Octavius,' later pictured as father-in-law of Magnus Maximus. Was the new throne ceded by the remnants of some fifth-century Dumnonian *ordo* to one whose family had been involved with the Roman purple? In the north, the various dynasts of the British kingdoms in southern Scotland have immediate ancestors whose names imply either partial Romanization, or the possession of titles associated with federate status. Did such families consider that previous recognition by Rome now advanced their special claims to tribal leadership? Some element of continuity, real or fictitious, seems inherent in at least some of these arrangements.

Not all the post-Roman kingdoms, as we must call them, are *civitates* in new guises. The Roman *civitas* in Britain was itself in all likelihood composed of con-

14

14 Rare silver coin of Caratacus (from Guildford, Surrey). Obverse, CARA and head of Hercules; reverse, eagle standing on serpent, with ring-ornament above. *c.* AD 35–40

stituent *pagi*, or subdistricts, and these must have been primarily native divisions. The word *pagus* survived to become Welsh *peu*, Cornish *pou*: Powys in North Wales is from *pagenses*, 'the people who dwell in the *pagus*'. There were subsidiary kings, *reguli* in later Latin writings; those of the Picts may have lain behind the *mormaers* or 'great stewards' of early medieval Scotland, and the usual Cornish word for 'king', *myghtern*, means originally something like 'vice-king'. It is tempting to imagine that remnants of the *pagus* system underlie numerous small kingdoms of which we know little beyond the mere names; Elmet, inland from York, or Deira (the Vale of York), or perhaps the hypothetical Bernaccia ('land of the mountain passes') in the Pennines and parts of Northumbria – as 'Deira' and 'Bernicia' the last two passed into the later kingdom of the Angles. There seem to have been others, in the eastern Cotswolds and in parts of Cheshire and South Lancashire. Unfamiliar as this complicated pattern may look within the context of England, it was (modified) the ancestral mosaic of land-division in the Celtic-speaking world, and could have been found throughout Ireland at this time; probably, too, north of the Antonine Wall among the Picts (who were in some fashion split between north and south, with seven sub-kingdoms). It need not surprise us to encounter, as we shall, such other echoes of prehistory as the reoccupation of Iron Age hill-forts, or the production of hand-made domestic pottery.

A Host of Tongues

Unlike the French, Spanish, Italians, and Romanians, the British do not speak a language descended from Latin. Why are we not heirs, like these other nations, to the speech of the legions and the Roman administrative machinery? The reasons are many, and a delicate balance must have been tipped by small considerations.

A Celtic language, British – ancestor of Welsh and Cornish – was current throughout England, Wales, and much of Scotland when the Romans arrived. Doubtless there were variations of dialect, since not all the constituent pre-Roman Iron Age peoples had arrived in Britain at the same period; but these need have been no greater than the extremes of difference encountered in rural English dialects now. British was the common speech, as the closely related Gaulish was in Gaul. Latin, a *lingua franca* essential to an army and a mercantile empire whose people were drawn from the homes of a hundred languages, became a second vernacular; the language of government, of trade, of culture and education, and above all the language of writing. Over the Roman centuries, hundreds of spoken Latin words were borrowed into British. Some were names of objects which had been unknown before the advent of the superior Roman technology (thus Welsh *ffenestr*, Cornish *fenester*, are from Latin *fenestra*, 'window'); others, for aspects of life in which the Romans were presumably better organized or produced better answers, must have replaced native words – thus Welsh *ysgol*, 'school' is from Latin *schola*, Late British *pont*, 'bridge', from Latin *pontem* (*pons*).

The removal of the official Roman military and civil presence, with the decline of officialdom and urban life, encouraged the reassertion of the native British speech. Spoken and written Latin survived, given added importance in post-Roman times through its universal rôle in Church life; this took Latin, as the tongue of both learning and religion, well into the Middle Ages. At the popular level, British, not Latin, took the brunt of linguistic attack from the Germanic world of the Angles, Saxons, and others. The tight group of Old English dialects evolved, through the selection of one of them as an eventual standard form, into Middle and Modern English; because of our own Imperial history, this became again the language of government and international commerce. The descendants of British, their minor differences emphasized through geographical isolation, became dialects and then languages. Cumbric or Cumbrian (British in the far north-west) died out only in Viking or Norman times; Cornish lasted until the Hanoverians: and Welsh survives today, on the defensive, but still a widely used popular speech. Across the Channel, Breton, as we shall see an implanted offshoot of south-west British, is under constant and deliberate attack by the French who, since the Buonapartes, have viewed non-French languages within France as potential vehicles of sedition rather than as legacies of history.

In Britain and Ireland between AD 400 and 800, the overall linguistic position was a complicated one. Celtic languages known to history all descend from a postulated prehistoric 'Common Celtic', which (this is naturally speculative) may have been diffused westwards from the Alpine region during the late second and the early first millennia BC. With this language-family we associate the (archaeologically detected) spread of iron metallurgy, of fortified hill-top settlement, and of aspects of horsemanship and wheeled vehicles.

Irish, still spoken in the Atlantic west of Ireland, and forcibly revived as an official second language in the Republic, descends from an elaborate and archaic speech current in post-Roman centuries, and presumably present in Ireland for many centuries before that. Our problem is that it is far from simple to declare which particular prehistoric settlement in Ireland, definable only in archaeological terms, could have introduced it. There is a growing tendency – reinforced by the character of Old Irish itself, which argues a comparatively early branching from the parent Common Celtic and Indo-European stock – to push this introduction well back in the first millennium BC, if not earlier.

Descendants in historic times of Irish are Manx, now extinct as a vernacular, which appears to have replaced a British speech in the Isle of Mann; and Scottish Gaelic, introduced through western Scotland by Irishmen from the fifth century AD onwards. These two have not diverged from the parent language to the extent seen in the case of Welsh, Cornish, and Breton, though to the layman this fact is partly obscured by the phonetic conventions employed to write Manx.

Scotland, north of the line from Edinburgh to Glasgow, was in post-Roman times the home of at least three languages, and this excludes any spoken Latin. There were, as we have just seen, Irish speakers in the west. In the east and the north were the Picts. By this period, the Picts were a mixture of former peoples; a very large element of Bronze Age, or earlier, aboriginals, and groups of Iron Age newcomers. The latter spoke what we know as 'Pictish P-Celtic', or 'Celtic Pictish', which can have differed but little from British – the differences stem from the separate history of the Iron Age in North Britain. The common place-name prefix 'Pit', as in Pitlochrie and Pittenweem, is Celtic Pictish *pett*, and is the same as the Latinized Gaulish loanword *petia*, whence (through French *pièce*), our own 'piece'. 'Pit' (*pett*) means just that; 'a piece' of land, a land-holding, a farm.

'Non-Celtic Pictish', on the other hand, known to us almost entirely from some personal names and rather late inscriptions on stone, may have survived until Viking times; but it is, or was, that linguistic rarity, a language whose very nature and relatives cannot be identified. There is little point in guessing, from so small a sample, whether it had anything to do with Basque or Eskimo; it must surely be a Bronze Age or Neolithic survival. Of phrases like *iddarrnonn vorrenn'ipuor*, the most one can say is that they probably contain some personal names.

Chapter Two

Invaders and Colonists

Hengist and Horsa

It has often been stressed that when we talk of 'the Roman garrison' or 'the withdrawal of most of the army in 407', any picture involving well-drilled ranks composed entirely of Italians is a totally false one. Increasingly, throughout the Late Roman period, the army in Britain, as elsewhere, had been drawn from non-Roman peoples, the British among them. The various Germans – Franks, Goths, Alemanni, and many other groups – figured largely in this, renowned for their martial qualities; notable generals, of whom Stilicho is but one, came from this background.

In addition to non-legionary auxiliary units, organized on such an ethnic basis, other varieties of defensive troops could be found. These are better known from Gaul and the Rhineland, as *laeti* and *foederati*. The federate soldiers in particular were members of tribes, under their own leaders, where the tribes were linked to Rome by *foederatio*, a technical process involving treaty relations and recognition.

That this applied to Roman Britain is clear from the reported presence of an Alemannic king, Fraomar, serving as a tribune with a large body of his countrymen somewhere in the 370s; Professor Sheppard Frere suggests here a force of *numeri*, tribal levies, rather than *foederati*. The existence of German soldiers, and this probably included Saxons as well as unspecified tribesmen, in and around many of the towns and settlements of Late Roman Britain is borne out by a whole series of metal objects –

15

15 Tombstone of a non-Roman cavalry-man (Rufus Sita, of the sixth Thracian Cohort) spearing a barbarian; Gloucester, first century AD

belt-buckles and other items of quasi-military uniform and equipment – which cover the fourth and earlier fifth centuries, and have also occurred in what seem to be
16 appropriate graves.

It is against this background that we must see the story of Vortigern, Hengist and Horsa. The version preserved

16 Bronze objects from grave I, Dyke Hills, Dorchester-on-Thames, Oxon; military burial, probably of a Germanic federate settler, from the end of Roman Britain

in that part of Nennius' compilation that can be supposed to rest (as John Morris argues) on a lost 'Kentish Chronicle' is supplemented by other versions derived from the writings of Gildas and Bede, and given a measure of chronology from European sources. Without involving detailed arguments as to date, the period from 425 to 450 is seen to be almost certain. Various barbarians, Irish from the west and the sea-raiding Picts on the east coast, were threatening the weak and disunited provinces of Roman Britain. Vortigern, not among 'the last of the Romans' or the surviving ruling caste of lowland sub-Roman Britain, but the most powerful of the native tyrants and one who sought to act as a national authority, implanted *foederati* of his own; as we shall see, it is possible that Vortigern lies behind a similar event in North Wales. Three shiploads of Saxons (who may, in fact, have been Scandinavian Jutes, and moreover at this time in Frisia) under Hengist and Horsa were induced to settle in the south-east – perhaps in Kent, perhaps, too, then, or in the guise of subsequent bands, in parts of East Anglia and around the Wash. Piratic Picts were to be repelled at sea by Germanic seamen of equal skill and ferocity.

The probability is that Vortigern acted, justifiably, as the Romans would have acted; our versions all come from those who were wise after the event. Either in one year, if so perhaps in 441 or 442, or over a generation, the Angles, Saxons, Jutes, and Frisians ceased merely to be *foederati* or *gentiles*, or any kind of controllable mercenary force, and struck out on their own account. Whether we can talk of 'a revolt', still less now of a mid-fifth-century 'arrival of the Saxons', is arguable. The picture of what had happened by 500 is still mainly pieced together from the detailed distribution-maps of Germanic cemeteries, 17 and over the fifth and sixth centuries it continues to be a series of generalized views.

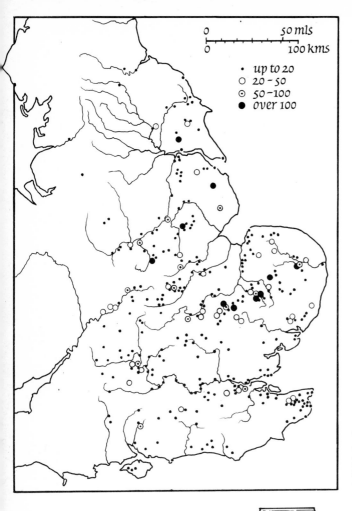

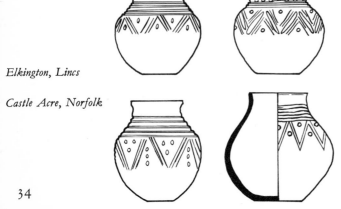

17, 18 An index of Germanic settlement; *left*, distribution of Anglo-Saxon pottery in the pagan Saxon period. *Below*, some direct comparisons between homelands and colonies.

Elkington, Lincs

Castle Acre, Norfolk

Westerwanna, Lower Saxony

Borgstedt, Schleswig-Holstein

19 Offa's Dyke, looking north. This English frontier against the Welsh, 120 miles of earthworks, dates from the end of the eighth century AD

34

There were cultural differences. Certain Germanic peoples cremated their dead; others buried them. Styles of pottery, known to us because they are so frequently found in graves, must be studied typologically not only in English settings, but with reference to contemporary styles in the postulated homeland areas. In the south, the advance westwards was, it would now seem clear, halted around 500 by a British victory, usually identified as that of Mount Badon, and was resumed three generations later in a constant pressure which was to end only with the building of Offa's Dyke and the eventual Wessex conquests of Cornwall, last remnant of Dumnonia. The various early English kingdoms – Kent, Wessex, East Anglia, Mercia, and those in the north – must have early roots, but in the form in which we are familiar with them they are shapings of the later sixth and seventh centuries.

At the level of the British countryside, what really took place? This remains a vast question-mark. Like the Celtic-speaking peoples, the Germans, save for the comparatively advanced Frankish groups in Kent, were not town-dwellers. Neither their technology nor their social structure predisposed them to this way of life. They lacked cavalry, and their rulers and thegns preferred timber halls to hill-forts. There is no real evidence that Anglo-Saxons made a practice of sacking Roman villas, still less that there were any occupied villas for them to sack. A characteristic view of Roman towns and Roman masonry is given by an Old English poem called *The Ruin*, a masterly fragment from an unnamed West Saxon bard; it probably alludes to the remains of Roman Bath. 'Wondrous is this wall-stone' it begins (R.K. Gordon's translation); 'Broken by fate, the castles have decayed; the work of giants is crumbling.' To the poet, such incredible work was something from an unimaginable past – between the mighty builders and his own time, surely 'a hundred generations of men have died.'

18

19

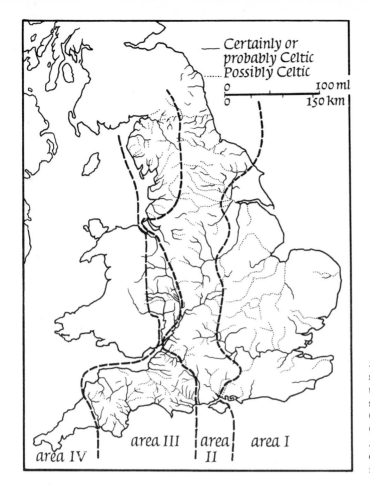

Certainly or
probably Celtic
........Possibly Celtic

| 0 | | 100 ml |
| 0 | | 150 km |

area IV   area III   area   area I
                       II

20 The 'River-
names' map, showing
the progressive
survival westwards of
Celtic, as opposed to
Germanic, names.
Area IV is almost
entirely Celtic in this
respect

One of the most vivid of the many maps which could
be used to illustrate the English settlements is Kenneth
Jackson's well-known map of river-names. In the place-
name field, it is known that certain basic and very simple
names, like those of hills and rivers, readily survive
colonization and linguistic change; extreme contrasts of
language, as in Australia and South Africa, admirably
display this trend. British river-names on the whole are
archaic, and may include some pre-Celtic labels; a high
proportion, when translatable, mean only 'river' or
'water' or some common adjective like 'dark', 'swift',

20

'muddy'. The map shows how, from east to west, the proportion of surviving Celtic river-names reflects in each area the appropriate linguistic dominance – from the east, Area I, in which only a handful of major names like Thames and Trent can be listed, to Area IV (Wales and Cornwall) where Germanic river-names are virtually absent. This is a refined conception, but it carries an earthy implication. The river- and stream-names were created, given, and used by the peoples of the fields and pastures, the peasants who took the land and tilled it; and perhaps no other map so fully demonstrates the real impact of the early English settlement.

Excursus: Arthur and Mount Badon

Who was King Arthur? The short and simple answer is, 'A character in fiction' – like Mr Micawber, or the Wife of Bath. Unfortunately this will not suffice; for the 'King Arthur' of medieval prose and verse, the light reading of their day, was drawn from the obscured half-memories of early history. If a moment's reflection shows us that at no point, in any authentic regnal list, is there a British monarch of this name recorded, another moment will convince us that the work of Tennyson, Sir Thomas Malory, and Geoffrey of Monmouth is unlikely to be rendered null and void by mere academic quibbles.

We can distinguish, at once, between 'King Arthur', creator and leader of the Knights of the Round Table, central pivot of all those tales about the Holy Grail, the concepts of chivalry, the unfortunate incests, the magical birth and the equally magical death and passing; and 'Arthur', the remote shadowy war-leader whose period, in so far as it can be fixed, centred around AD 500. It is this latter man, not a king but some kind of soldier-hero, who must concern us.

Arthur's date is usually fixed because of its association – a link too strong to be seriously questioned – with a battle at somewhere called Mons Badonicus, 'Mount Badon', and if the date of *this* is still argued, it is agreed to fluctuate between about 500 and 520. If this be so, we have no contemporary reference to the hero himself. All the allusions older than 1136, when Geoffrey of Monmouth produced the first full-scale elaboration of the 'King Arthur' of legend, were collected and discussed recently by Professor Thomas Jones. It may surprise those who regard the original Arthur as somehow a Cornishman, or who think that 'Camelot' was in Somerset, to learn that the earliest references take us firmly to North Britain.

In strict historical terms, there are two separate ideas; the battle of Mount Badon, and the war-leader Arthur. Mount Badon was a real and notable event, mentioned about 540 by Gildas (who does not name Arthur) in terms suggesting that it had taken place a generation earlier. In the *Annales Cambriae*, a North British chronicle first put together from older material in the mid-tenth century, it is dated to 516 (or 518), and Arthur *is* named as the victor; but this additional fact could well have been inserted at a later date – as late as the final redaction, about 1100. A detail about the British having carried the Cross of Our Lord on their shoulders seems to have been borrowed from a supposed 'List of Arthur's Twelve Battles' in the ninth-century compilation by the Welsh monk Nennius; here, it is actually the image of the Blessed Virgin, the battle in question is 'Caer Guinnion' (unlocated), the confusion between two Old Welsh words for 'shoulder' and 'shield' (in modern Welsh, *ysgwydd* and *ysgwyd* respectively) is almost certain, and Nennius' tale has all the hallmarks of an eighth- or ninth-century ecclesiastical legend.

Arthur, the original form of whose name (*Artorius*?) need not bother us unduly, was some sort of early British hero. What may be the oldest reference to him is a terse

entry in the *Annales Cambriae*, under the year 537 (or
539): 'The battle of Camlann, in which Arthur and
Medraut were slain.' Camlann may be a late form of
21 *Camboglanna*, a fort (near the modern Birdoswald) on
Hadrian's Wall. Our first *poetic* reference also comes from
the North. In a remarkable verse epic known as the
Gododdin, attributed to the poet Aneirin, we learn of a
British war-band from the region of Edinburgh, who
rode down Dere Street to 'Catraeth' (Catterick, near
Richmond, in Yorkshire) in order to fight the Northumbrian Angles. All were slain, save for the poet and one
other. The poem is a lament, and of profound importance
as one of the oldest of its kind in European literature:
Sir Ifor Williams' demonstration that the core of it does
indeed date from about 600 is accepted. The allusion we
seek comes in two lines – 'He glutted black ravens on the
wall of the fortress, Though he was not Arthur' – and
seems to mean that the man described, Gwarddur, was a
brave fighter, if not in Arthur's class. Unhappily this
couplet occurs in a verse which, from the spelling, could
be an addition of the ninth century; but it is not entirely
beyond question as an original passage of about 600. It
confirms the historicity of Arthur, because (as Professor
Jones points out) there are no references to legendary or
unhistorical figures elsewhere, and many of those named
in the poem are independently attested.

The list of Arthur's twelve battles given by Nennius is
of little help. Only four (apart from Mount Badon) can
be even loosely located; one seems to be Chester, another
is possibly in Lincolnshire, and the other two are probably in southern Scotland. It is most unlikely that the
historical Arthur fought in all these engagements, even if
he was involved in one or more of them. When the
Annales Cambriae was finally redacted (after 1100), Arthur,
the successful general of bygone glories, and Mount
Badon, long known to be the last and greatest of battles

against the English, were placed together – under the year 516 (or 518), which must be approximately correct. For this does not conflict with the other entry, seemingly independent, concerning Arthur's death at Camlann in 537 (or 539); and this may be right, too. Indeed, Arthur could have been the victorious leader at Mount Badon, wherever that was; and many people think that this is in accord with the idea of a roving general, whose band of armed horsemen would merely anticipate the tactics described in the *Gododdin* poem. But we cannot escape the hard fact that pre-medieval references to Arthur are categorically northern, and that the British tribes in what is now southern Scotland may have formed his native background. His adoption as a universal British hero would inevitably have dispersed his fame over the whole range of British speech, British story-telling, and British resistance to the Saxon. This must be why, later, we find Arthurian stories – and even places – in Cumbria, Wales, and Cornwall. In exactly this fashion, other not dissimilar epic tales spread south, like that of Tristan, Isolde, and the wicked uncle King Mark; originally North British, or even (Celtic) Pictish – *Drust* (Tristan) was a common

21 Camboglanna (Birdoswald, Cumberland); the Roman fort on Hadrian's Wall, looking north. The river Irthing appears in the foreground

Pictish name – this saga had reached Cornwall, to be relocated in the neighbourhood of Fowey and Castle Dore, not long before Norman poets found it and worked it up into the tragic romance which ended its career in Wagner's opera.

Where, then, was Mount Badon? Where, in the south of England, are the British likely to have halted a westward Saxon advance shortly after 500? Numerous localities, mostly with the syllable Bad – in their names, have been 22 suggested, and present opinion favours Badbury Rings in Dorset, a massive Iron Age hill-fort near an important Roman road. That it was a successful British victory is not in doubt; it may have halted the Saxons for half a century, and Gildas' words imply that a phase of stability, of relative security, and of orderly government, followed the victory and persisted until his own day. Gildas also refers to *rectores*, where *rector* is (and presumably still carried that implication then) the title of a Roman provincial governor. Were there attempts to revive the institutions of the fourth century and of sub-Roman times? Whether the slow collapse of this lowland British world, after the 550s, was due to the renewed Saxon advance, or (as Gildas may be thought to hint) to the disruptive quarrels of *duces*, war-leaders and would-be Arthurs connected with the network of native principalities to the west and north, or to both factors, we can do little more than guess; but the names of Arthur, and of the battle of the Badonic Mount, had passed immutably into the popular tradition of the British people.

Painted Men in the North

A minor but interesting event, of which very little is known or has been written, is the limited expansion of the Picts during the sixth and seventh centuries – the evidence 35 suggests the formation of scattered colonies in Orkney and Shetland, and perhaps Skye.

We have previously noted the Picts in regard to their languages. Historically, we can speak of the Picts – *Picti* or 'Painted Ones', as the Roman legionaries seem to have labelled them – only from AD 297, when this term is first recorded, to the mid-ninth century, when, during the reign of Kenneth mac Alpin, any political identity which the Picts still possessed was swallowed up in their amalgamation with the Scots, descendants of the fifth-century Irish colonists in the west. Of course this can hardly imply that there were no Picts before 297. The Picts were, as we saw, a composite people, descendants of the Bronze Age and even earlier inhabitants of north-east Scotland from the Moray Firth to the Forth, and of various Iron Age groups – possibly from as far back as certain fort-building elements of the sixth century BC – who had settled among them.

22 Mons Badonicus? An aerial view of the hill-fort known as Badbury Rings, Dorset, perhaps the leading claimant to this title

In attempting to map the homeland of the Picts, we can use a number of distribution-maps, and see how far they coincide. The division between northern and southern Picts, which was certainly regarded as real in Bede's day,
23 was imposed by the ridge of high country, the Mounth, that runs east–west to the sea near Aberdeen. The place-
24 name element *Pit* ('piece of land, farm') is perhaps the best basis for the latter centuries of Pictland, and its spread can interestingly be compared to an archaeo-
25–7 logical map of souterrains – underground chambers, usually attached to dwellings, artificially and carefully constructed and used for such purposes as byres and food-stores. Souterrains in Scotland were current in the second century AD but, as in Ireland, there is evidence that they were in use for some centuries after that. Elsewhere in Britain and Ireland, the introduction of souterrains is associated with Iron Age newcomers and if, as the Scottish distribution rather implies, this type of construction was particularly associated with the Picts, we can regard it as in some way introduced by Celtic-speaking *Picti*.

23 *Left*, the Mounth; a view at Glen Esk, Angus. This east–west ridge of high ground and glens divided the northern and southern Picts

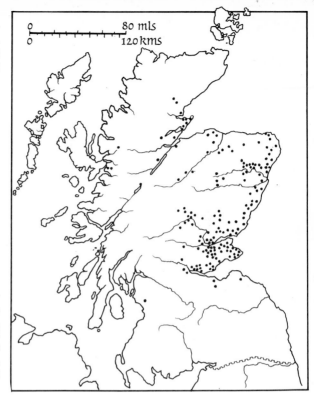

24 Distribution of the place-name element *Pit-*, earlier *Pett*, 'piece of land, landholding, farm'. The markedly restricted occurrence of this element defines, albeit very generally, the extent of Pictish settled land-use in the period 300–800

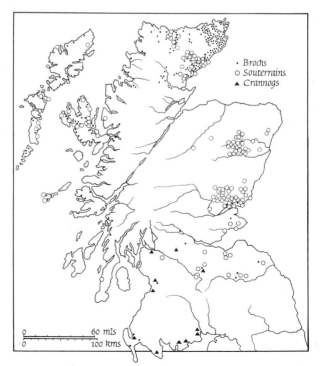

25 Selected types of field-monument in the Roman Iron Age of Scotland; within this by no means uniform distribution, souterrains may bear some relation to early Pictish settlement. Note the outlying groups of souterrains in the north-east, Skye and the Outer Isles

- Brochs
- ○ Souterrains
- ▲ Crannogs

26, 27 *Above*, main passage of the large stone-walled souterrain at Carn Euny, west Cornwall (? first century BC). If, as seems likely, the habit of constructing souterrains spread from south to north along Atlantic Britain and Ireland, Pictish souterrains (like that at Ardestie, Angus, *below*) should fall well within the Roman centuries; excavated finds from Ardestie tend to bear out this estimate

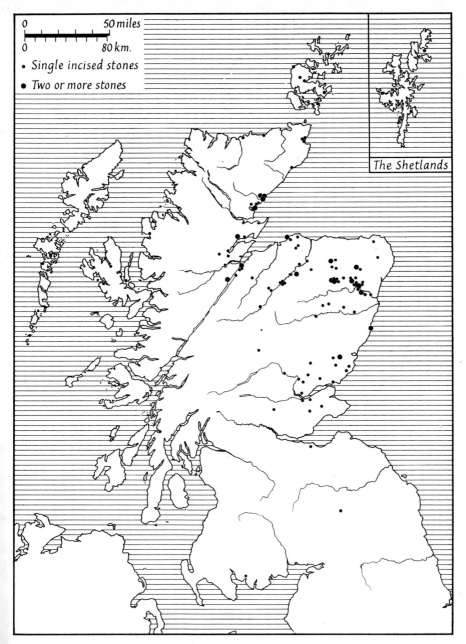

28 Distribution of stone slabs and boulders bearing incised Pictish symbols (*cf. ills* 29–32) of Class I – pre-Christian, sixth and probably fifth centuries A D. An origin-centre in northern Pictland is implied. Note the similarity to the *Pit*- and souterrain maps (*ills.* 24, 25)

30–32 Pictish slabs with Class I symbols. *Left*, Glamis Manse: Snake, Fish, Mirror. *Centre*, Dunnichen, Angus: 'Flower' symbol, Double Disc and Z-Rod, Comb and Mirror. *Right*, Easterton of Roseisle: Goose over Fish (salmon). The first two can be interpreted as pictorial tombstones, perhaps commemorations by surviving womenfolk (if Mirror and Comb= 'wife'). The Bird/Fish motif occurs, however, four times on Pictish Class I stones, and may carry some other significance; early European parallels hint at a cult-scene

29　The Pictish bestiary (Class I symbols). The 'Horse's Head', *lower left*, may be an incomplete red deer; the 'Stag' is a reindeer. Above his rump: the 'Elephant'

The most important map, and the one which is generally linked to that of names starting with Pit-, is that of so-called 'Class I symbol stones'. Archaeology has so far been able to tell us remarkably little about the Picts, but one point on which there is unlikely now to be doubt is that certain groups of carved and shaped stones are Pictish handiwork, and no one else's. These stones – at first, often mere boulders or slabs or pillars, even occasional outcrops, but later tending to be roughly shaped – bear groups of (usually) one to four symbols, incised in outline through a technique of pocking a line and then smoothing it to a shallow curved channel (a technique which, over much of North Britain, goes far back into Bronze Age times). The symbols are already stereotyped when we encounter them – variation is confined to

28

29–32

internal ornament rather than to any change of shape –
and can be classified as living creatures (animals, birds, a
snake, a fish); simple and elaborate geometrical shapes;
and a number of depictions of real objects (mirror, comb,
sword) shown whole or in part or occasionally from
unfamiliar angles.

These are the Class I stones. Class II stones, which are
not only more regularly shaped, but exhibit a wide range
of Christian symbols, even scenes with figures, executed
in relief technique as well as the incised (pocked and
reamed) lines, clearly post-date the Picts' conversion to
Christianity. This is associated with Christian missionary
work based on the Scotic colonies in the west, in the late
sixth and seventh centuries, and the Class I stones are thus
presumably (a) earlier – sixth century, and very probably
fifth, and (b) specifically non-Christian.

The only hypothesis which really covers these monuments – and it receives support by analogy from much
of the Old World before, at, and after this period – is that
Pictish symbol-stones are tombstones. Class I stones may

have been inspired by the pictorial element of (non-Christian) Roman altars and memorial tombstones, familiar enough to Picts and Caledonians over several centuries of frontier warfare. I have argued elsewhere that the (dominant ?) Celtic-speaking class in Pictish society was responsible for this innovation. The Picts were, until some time after their conversion, non-literate, and possessed no script to write either of their languages. They used pictorial designs on gravestones to indicate, not individual names, but such generalized ideas as status, occupation, and some form of tribal descent (there are fourteen 'animal' symbols, perhaps related to the idea, recorded in medieval Scottish sources, that Pictland had seven constituent provinces, each with a king and under-king).

The other symbols include some which appear to be derived, at some remove, from the Bronze Age 'cup-and-ring' markings of the area, and others which depict objects proper to the Iron Age material culture of England and lowland Scotland before and during the earlier Roman centuries. Their continued currency until post-Roman times might be due to an unbroken tradition of employment as personal tattoo markings – there are a number of classical allusions to this as a Pictish custom, on the face as well as the body, and it probably underlies the nickname *Picti*.

The historical Picts' northernmost province was the ancient Catanesia, the east coast of Ross and the county of Caithness. This may in itself indicate a northward spread in, or shortly after, the late Roman period. What concerns us now is the presence of this strange funerary art in outlying islands.

In Orkney and Shetland, there are some half-dozen symbol stones, one of them – conjoined with a picture of three men – a Christian grave-slab. To this we should add some objects of bone and stone from excavated sites in

35 Silver strap-terminals, eighth century AD, from the St Ninian's Isle (Shetland) hoard. Art from the Northern Isles at this period has Pictish and Northumbrian, rather than Irish, roots

33, 34

36, 37

both groups, relevant because they appear to belong to secondary occupation of brochs and wheel-houses of the period contemporary with Roman times further south, and they should belong to pre-Norse times. We recall here that when St Columba of Iona visited the Pictish king, Bridei son of Maelcon, at the royal fortress near Inverness he was concerned for the safety of Irish missionaries in the Northern Isles; the *regulus* or 'sub-king' of Orkney was at Bridei's court and Bridei then held hostages from this prince, which implies a measure of control. This was late in the sixth century. Lastly, the name of the Pentland Firth comes from the Old Norse form, *Pettalandsfjordr*, 'the firth of the land of the Picts', and numerous place-names in Orkney and Shetland with the prefix *Petta* ('of the Picts') suggest that this ascription had some meaning in the eighth century.

In the large island of Skye, there is an isolated group of five symbol stones, and one each on the isles of Benbecula and Pabbay, across the Minch. On a visit to Skye, St Columba once baptized an aged person called Artbranan, to whom he was obliged to speak through an interpreter, and who was leader of a cohort or war-band; the adjective 'Geona' applied to his cohort might suggest Ce, one of the east-coast Pictish provinces, and Artbranan is a Celtic (Celtic Pictish?) name. The distribution-map of Scottish souterrains also shows an isolated cluster on Skye, and there are some on North and South Uist. That Skye has in some way a history which differs slightly from the general west-coast picture is actually borne out by recent work on blood-group distributions, and the highest values of the gene A – which are, however, usually associated with later Norse colonists – occur in Skye, Orkney, the Moray Firth, and parts of Caithness, according to Dr Elizabeth Brown's survey.

The First Scots

From south-west Scotland to north-east Ireland is a short sea passage – there are people in the Rinns of Galloway whose parents shopped, by steam-packet, in Ulster! – and it is possible to travel along the west Scottish coast, in relative safety, as far north as Oban and Mull. To this Argyllshire seaboard came fifth-century settlers from Dal Riata, a district of County Antrim. These, the *Scoti* or *Scotti* (in origin, an uncomplimentary label) of St Patrick's writings and later of Bede's, traditionally set out as an organized migration; Fergus son of Erc, his three sons, and a fleet with 150 men. Adomnán's *Life of St Columba*, written in the 680s, looks back at the ruling class of these Dalriadic Scots a century earlier.

36, 37 *Left*, St Columcille, or Columba, of Iona; detail from a ninth-century MS. of Adamnan's Life of Columba (*c.* 690). *Right*, small bronze head (27 mm) from excavations of the Iona monastery – perhaps intended to portray a monastic brother (? seventh or eighth century)

38 The rock of
Dunadd, western
Argyll. The
small citadel,
stronghold of Irish
settlers, occupies the
low summit

Armed conflict is a commonplace in the medieval, and
pre-medieval, references to this colonization. Fortified
coastal strongholds like Dunadd, by the Crinan Canal, and
Dunollie, overlooking Oban Harbour, symbolize its
nature. These first Scots spoke the Irish of their homeland, until the tenth century the same language, and only
differentiating into Scottish Gaelic after the early Middle
Ages. Does this mean that, in the long coastal belt of
Argyll and in the islands offshore, they encountered a
landscape bereft of both British and Picts? We cannot
be sure, but this is still a region which, after another
fourteen centuries, can hardly be described as over-
crowded.

The later history of the Dalriadic settlement – after the
ninth century – becomes that of medieval Scotland itself.
There is a limited amount of archaeological evidence.
Dunadd, an odd little isolated hill crowned by a complex
citadel with outworks, was one of the first strongholds –
in St Columba's day, apparently the most important – and
was most incompetently dug many years ago. The finds
include some small objects which would generally be
regarded as Irish. In the ancestral country, Antrim is one
of the very few parts of Early Christian Ireland where
40, 41 domestic handmade pottery was in use at this time.
Known, a trifle inaccurately, as 'souterrain ware', this
pottery, which represents a surviving tradition first
brought to northern Ireland in the Iron Age from somewhere in Britain, is peculiar in that the undersides of the

bases bear the impressions of chopped dried grass, incorporated into the vessel's surface because the damp pots were stood to dry on this material, and then fired out, leaving the negative imprint. Sherds of this kind have been found in early levels at Iona, where a monastery was established in AD 563 by St Columba and his companions in order to minister to their fellow Irish in the region; and other, similar, sherds have come from a couple of small islands in the Sound of Harris, in the Outer Hebrides. Missionary activity, rather than agricultural pioneering, is indicated here.

An admirable guide to the early Irish settlement could be constructed from the distribution of certain place-name elements – particularly those relating to simple natural features – which can be shown to be early, to exhibit a usage which differs from British, Pictish, or later Scottish Gaelic, and (presumably) to have been first given currency by Irish colonists. One well-known instance

39 A Pictish seagirt stronghold? Dunnottar Rock, on the east Scottish coast, was subsequently used for a medieval castle

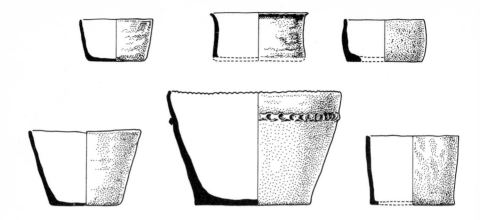

40, 41 *Above*, 'Souterrain ware' from north-east Ireland; the cordoned vessel, *centre*, is a local development. *Below*, 'Grass-marked ware' from sites in west Cornwall. Both hand-made groups bear fired-out impressions of chopped dried grass; both fall within the period AD 400–800. The Cornish pots, intrusive in the local ceramic sequence, point to actual colonization from the north of Ireland, probably starting in the late sixth century AD

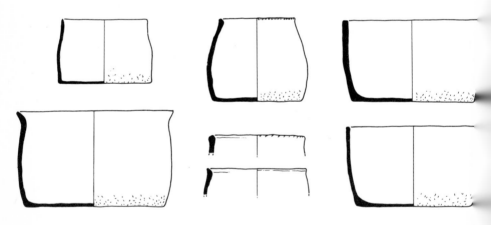

42 concerns a word *sliabh*, which in Ireland means 'mountain', but in Scotland can describe a hillock or even just high ground (often in the Anglicized form of Slew-). The pattern relates very neatly, as Professor Nicolaisen has shown, to the first Dalriadic settlement-area, but it is surprising to find an intense localized concentration in the double peninsula of the Rinns of Galloway, opposite Antrim.

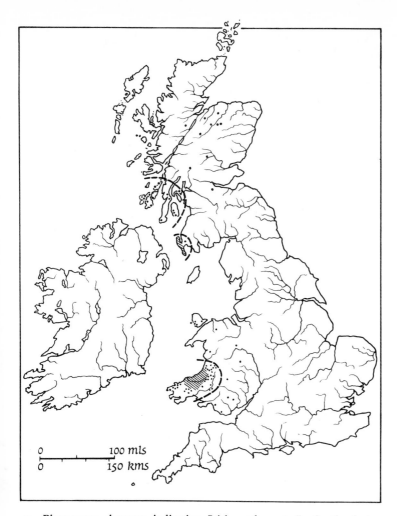

42 Place-name elements indicating Irish settlement. In Scotland the Irish *sliabh* ('mountain'); in Wales, *meidr*, *moydir*, dialect words for 'lane', may be modelled on Irish usage

No special historical sources describe what now looks like another early Irish colony here – possibly of the sixth century. But isolated archaeological finds from Galloway, the spread of a type of early ecclesiastical site (the enclosed developed cemetery) which may be regarded as Irish-inspired, and several minor pointers in the same direction, are amounting to reliable evidence for a separate settlement in this south-western area.

Irishmen in Mann and Wales

The Manx language, like Scottish Gaelic, is a transplanted Irish speech. The early historic archaeology of Mann, notably that part dealing with Christianity, goes very markedly with Ireland rather than Britain; even the basic Manx name *keeill* for an early chapel site with its surrounding cemetery is simply the Irish *cill*. On the other hand, certain aspects of Manx archaeology in the Iron Age, and of the period parallel to the Roman centuries in Britain, looks east rather than west for parallels. The evidence that the Manx were, until some unspecified post-Roman horizon, British-speaking depends on the interpretation of some place-names, and on an interesting memorial stone from Andreas, in the north of the Island. This – dated to about 500 – is bilingual, giving the name of the dead man and his father in both British and primitive Irish forms. In the ninth century, a North Welsh king, Merfyn Frych son of Gwriad (acceded 825), seems to have come from Mann, and his father's British name may appear on a ninth-century cross-slab from Mann bearing the words CRUX GURIAT. We may have here evidence of an Irish colony, commencing about the time of those in Scotland, and destined to absorb, linguistically, the native population.

43

44

Beyond Mann lies the long Lancashire coast. It is true that, among a number of small objects of post-Roman date found in the Wirral Peninsula of Cheshire, and further inland, there are some which might be argued to be of Irish origin; and at Heysham, the ruins of the ninth-century (?) St Patrick's Chapel, on a small rocky promontory and with some rock-cut graves west of it, might be thought to continue an even older Irish Christian foundation. For lack of evidence, we must however continue southwards to Wales.

Irish settlement in Wales is, as one might expect, most marked in those areas closest to Ireland. In the north-

43, 44   *Left*, the Calf of Man Crucifixion – a slate altar-frontal panel, eighth century, inspired by Irish metalwork? (*cf. ill.* 67). *Right*, the CRUX GURIAT cross-slab (ninth century), may commemorate the Manx father of a Welsh king

west, these are Anglesey, and the long 'pig's ear' – the Llyn Peninsula of Caernarvonshire; in the south-west, the 'pig's snout', the modern Pembroke with its flanking countries of Cardigan and Carmarthen. The relative accessibility of the whole South Wales coastal plain must be linked with traces of yet another minor settlement in the modern county of Brecknock or Brecon – traditionally, so named from an Irish king, Brychan (*Brocagnus*).

The place-name Llyn (older, Lleyn), and one or two others in that area – Dinllaen, Mallaen – have long been explained as containing the nominative plural or genitive plural forms of a word *Lagin*, or *Laigin*, an Irish collective term 'Leinstermen'. If so, they point to settlement from directly across the Irish Sea. Now various pieces of evidence suggest that this may have been among the earliest migrations of Irishmen, perhaps well back in the Roman era, becoming an established fact by the fourth century. Caernarvonshire, like other regions of highland Britain, is marked by the presence of distinctive home-steads known as 'enclosed hut groups' – two or more living-huts contained within a tight surrounding wall, a prototype farmhouse cluster. At least three specific forms of this appear to have no predecessors or obvious parallels anywhere in Wales. Our knowledge of the field-archaeo-logy of Ireland is by no means wide, but recent aerial survey makes it slightly more feasible that these could be the homes of the Irish settlers, and we recall the traditional Welsh term *cwtiau'r Gwyddelod* – 'cots of the *Goidels*, or Irish' – for these abandoned hut-circles.

Associated with this North Welsh episode is one of the strangest aspects of sub-Roman history. Certain semi-Romanized peoples on the fringes of the Roman provinces were admitted by treaty (*foedus*) into the status known as *foederatio*; they were, as we saw, recognized under their own rulers (who often assumed Roman names or titles), were obliged to keep peace, and in return for various benefits were charged with the notional defence of a stretch of frontier – hiring poachers to turn gamekeepers, in other words. It is hard to believe that something of this sort did not underlie the transfer, under its ruler Cunedda and his sons, of most of a North British tribe from the Edinburgh-Stirling region to some part of north-west Wales. These people, in Welsh the *Gododdin*, successors to the late Iron Age *Votadini* around the southern shore of the Firth of Forth, were later said to have expelled the Irish from various parts of Wales; and such a function would best explain this odd move. The problem is to decide whether this took place in a late fourth-century Roman *milieu* – was it arranged by Stilicho, for instance ? – or, if later, in the fifth century (which can be argued). If so, it might constitute evidence for the widespread power of some 'over-king' like Vortigern among the revived native principalities.

Irish settlement in south-west Wales can be defined in several ways. Certain place-name elements – a dialect word (*meid(i)r, moydir*) for a farm-lane, another for a hillock (*cnwc*) – have been discussed by Professor Melville Richards, and their distributions seem to coincide, not only with the revived kingdom of Dyfed, historically in Irish hands in post-Roman times, but with such other features as memorial stones inscribed in the Irish ogam

45, 46   Irishmen who died overseas. *Left*, *Votecorix* (in British, *Voteporix*), king of Demetia (south-west Wales), *c.* AD 550. *Right*, *Quenataucus*, son of *Dinuus*, an Irishman in west Cornwall, *c.* AD 600.

alphabet, or bearing specifically Irish personal names, or even set out in a vertical fashion influenced by ogam writing.

Behind this lies an early Irish epic, known in a number of versions, called *The Expulsion of the Déisi*. The Déisi, in origin an unfree people who were subject to a long history of what we would now call racial persecution, migrated *en masse* from south-east Ireland to Pembroke, under a king whose recorded name (Eochaid Allmuir, 'Eochaid Over-Sea') heads their subsequent dynasty. The genealogy or regnal list, down to the seventh and eighth centuries, is preserved in both Irish and Welsh sources (one likes to think, independently), and includes the Guotepir or Voteporix addressed about 540 by Gildas. This king's tombstone, with his name in British and

Irish ogam, still survives. In some fashion linked with this migration was that of another Munster tribe, the Ui Liathain ('Sons, or Descendants, of Liathan'), who may have settled west of the Déisi in the Gower and west Glamorgan.

It was once fashionable to place this happening back to the early third century, but a cautious reassessment from the regnal list points rather to the end of the fourth century: Seamus Pender's suggestion that this may be connected with Magnus Maximus' withdrawal of the troops, including presumably any Welsh garrisons, in 383 is a weighty one. There had long been contact between south-west Wales and southern Ireland – some of it peaceful, even perhaps Christian, and the invention of the ogam stroke-alphabet lies in this context – but some of it was concerned with Irish piracy and raiding. We can follow Leslie Alcock in seeing, if to an undefined extent, the Irish slave-raiders and casual adventurers of the third and fourth centuries becoming permanent immigrants by the fifth, as they may earlier have become in the north-west. There are again certain small finds from a number of South Wales sites which do seem, in our present state of knowledge, to be peculiarly Irish.

The Far South-West

Below Wales, the long peninsula of south-west Britain points out into the Atlantic, from the Somerset coast to Land's End and Scilly. The high rocky cliffs are broken at various points by river-outlets, natural harbours, and stretches of sand-dunes (the Cornish 'towans'), and over much of its length this northern coastline looks towards Ireland as well as to South Wales.

We can dismiss the connection of St Patrick with Glastonbury in the Somerset levels, exposed by Professor Herbert Finberg as a medieval myth; and there is extremely little evidence to support ideas of Irish settlement

along the north coast of Somerset, except in the odd isolated pocket. In Cornwall, however, the tradition of Irish
immigrants – notably in the field of Christianity – has
not only lasted until today, but appears to be historically
based.

An intellectual southern Irish viewpoint is expressed
in the so-called 'Glossary' of Cormac mac Cuilennain
(831–903), at once prince and bishop of Cashel, Co.
Tipperary. This work, a kind of haphazard encyclopaedia,
recites some long-anterior tradition that the Irish had
once settled in south-west Britain, and it goes so far as to
name two fortresses (they may, actually, be one and the
same place) giving both British and Irish forms of the
names. The latter, *dind map Lethain*, or *dún maic Liatha[i]n*,
'Fortress of the Sons of Liathan', contains the same Irish

47, 48   One stone, three Irishmen (slab from Ivybridge, south Devon).
Earliest is the ogam, SUAQQUCOS (late sixth century); then FANONUS,
inscribed on the same face. On the reverse, *right*, SAGRANUUS, early
seventh century

tribal appellation, that of the Ui Liathain, that we found in South Wales. It is specifically located 'in the lands of the Cornish Britons', and it would be a help to be able to identify it. But this hint of a connection with South Wales is enough to direct our attention to the eastern half of Cornwall, the ring of agricultural land all round Bodmin Moor, extending across the Tamar into the west of south Devon.

47, 48 Here, we find a scattered group of inscribed memorial stones – some in Irish ogam and Latin letters, some in Latin letters alone but with Irish, not British, names – which begin in the latter part of the fifth century. For what it is worth, we should note that much of this area coincides with a large group of parishes whose patron saints, with patrons of isolated chapels and even holy wells, can be linked as 'The Children of Brychan', the legendary twenty-four children of the Irish king who founded Brecon; and that in Wales similar dedications are found over a wide south-central area, centred on Brecon and its surrounding valleys.

If we allow an east Cornwall/west Devon Irish settlement, connected with the fifth-century Irish in South Wales as well as with Ireland, we can also point to a separate, and apparently slightly later, settlement in the very west of Cornwall and in Scilly. Here, the medieval (and modern) traditions of 'Irish' patron saints amount to little, except that, interestingly, they look to Ulster and Leinster rather than, as with Wales, to Munster (the south of Ireland). Our clues are mainly archaeological. Cornwall *49, 50* was the western constituent of the *civitas* of the Dumnonii in Roman times, and in the post-Roman kingdom of Dumnonia it formed a distinct region with an area-name like *Cornovia* or *Cornuvia* (later, Cornubia). Relatively untouched by Roman commerce and technology, the farmers and tin-streamers of this remote land continued, through Roman and post-Roman times, to produce their

49, 50 Chieftains in post-Roman Dumnonia. *Left*, the *Men Scryfys* ('written stone') in the Land's End peninsula – tomb of RIALOBRANUS. *Right*, the Doniert Stone (near Liskeard, Cornwall) may have been set up by 'Dumnarth rex Cerneu id est Cornubiae', drowned in AD 875

own handmade pottery. This is one of the very few areas where we possess a complete pottery sequence from the Iron Age to the Middle Ages, and it is therefore one of considerable archaeological importance.

In a number of (peasant) homestead sites, this pottery sequence is interrupted culturally. The west Cornish sub-Roman pottery, called 'Gwithian-style' after the type-site, exhibits a range of well-made and hard-fired jars and platters derived from local Roman period vessels. At a stage which is estimated, on several grounds, to be in the later sixth century, pots of a very different fabric, shape, and technique appear. These have grass-marked undersides, and so closely resemble the 'souterrain ware' of Ulster in early Christian times that (as at Iona, and the two Hebridean sites) we can only regard them as due to Irish settlers. The problem is that souterrain ware occurs mainly in the modern Cos. Down and Antrim, and we have to postulate a fairly long passage, all the way from the north-east Irish coast to the Land's End peninsula. But small tools and ornaments which find their only known parallels in Ireland occur on these Cornish sites. Again, too, there is at least one Cornish place-name element – *bounder*, meaning 'a farm-lane' – which has an appropriately western distribution. Like the Welsh dialect *meidr*, *moydir*, it may ultimately go back to a meaning 'cow land' – the modern Irish word for a road, *bóthar*, goes back to a primitive form meaning 'cow-passage' – and it could indicate some mode of land-usage first popularized by Irish farmers and stockbreeders.

We have seen, by this stage, late Roman and post-Roman Irish settlements over most of Atlantic Britain. In western Scotland and Mann, they were sufficiently dense to introduce the Irish language; in Wales (where Dyfed was probably a bilingual area for centuries) and Cornwall, personal names and place-names mark a less intense linguistic imprint. It is by no means improbable that, during the fifth and sixth centuries AD, the sum total of Irish settlers and their families in western Britain equalled or even exceeded that of the various Germanic tribes on Britain's eastern and southern shores. The fact that so few general histories of Britain allude to these Irish settlements is because historians and archaeologists concerned with Ireland and western Britain at this period seldom bother to popularize their results or their views, and we get an unbalanced picture. The precise reasons for these settlements are a matter of conjecture – they can hardly have been as clear-cut as those of later Irish losses following, for example, potato famines – and they may be very complicated. The case of the Déisi is one of the migration of a dispossessed tribe; there may have been others. But population pressure within a static social system, conflicts between farmer and stockbreeder, finite amounts of Irish land available for either way of life, and the continued dynastic wars in early Ireland, must all be

kept in mind. What we know (or can deduce) of internal
Irish history in the heroic age, before Christianity became
dominant in the later sixth and seventh centuries, depicts
very much this state of affairs.

To Armorica and Beyond

The bonds between Cornwall and Brittany, the rugged
Atlantic peninsulas of Britain and France, have always
been close. Cornish and Breton were in the Middle Ages
regarded as virtually the same language, subsequent
divergence being largely a matter of spelling and pro-
nunciation (Breton, under French influence, replaces the
'th' heard in 'this' or 'think' by a 'z', etc.). The following
couplet demonstrates this:

(Cornish) *An gwella bara dhe dhybry*
A vyth gwaynys ow whesa
(Breton) *Ar gwellan bara da zebriñ*
A vez gounezet o c'hwieziñ
('The best bread to eat, Will be won with sweat'.)

Sixteenth-century Cornish parish registers contain
numerous references to Breton settlers, the modern
surname 'Britton' (Britten, Brittan) representing some of
their descendants. As late as the early nineteenth century,
Penzance gentry were still sending their sons to Brittany
to learn French, and French ways; and during the last war
Breton refugees ran a school in Newlyn, near Penzance.
Many Cornish and Breton place-names are straightforward doublets of each other (Landewednack, Lande-
vennec).

The basis of this relationship really began in the fifth
century AD. Armorica, 'the land by the sea', as the old
Gallo-Roman province now represented by Brittany was
called, had a long and contentious history, starting with
the revolt of the Venetic tribe against Julius Caesar in the
first century BC. Apart from its coastal belt, it may not

have been heavily populated, and certainly held several vast forests. Two continental writers, Sidonius Apollinaris (d. 489) and the Goth, Jordanes, writing in 551, refer to an episode of about 470, when a large band of British – said to number 12,000 men, under their king Riothamus or Riotimus – came over to France at the request of the Emperor Anthemius (467–72) in order to fight the Visigoths, by then established over much of southern Gaul. This appears to be historical, the British contingent subsequently settling on the Loire, at the easternmost fringe of Brittany.

What followed was that, during the rest of the fifth, the sixth, and perhaps even early seventh centuries AD, immigrants from south-west Britain continued to move to Armorica. The very name 'Brittany' commemorates this, as do the early divisions of that province – Dumnonia, and that which became Cornouailles (the third, Bro Werec, takes its name from a sixth-century ruler, Waroc). The exact course of this prolonged migration has been argued, on historical and linguistic grounds, by Kenneth Jackson. Starting with, doubtless, the families and kinsfolk of Riothamus' war-bands, who may have been drawn from a wide area of southern Britain, the subsequent movement was derived from Devon and Cornwall; and the close correspondence between the two languages, Cornish and Breton, implies that it was the speech of the later (sixth-century) immigrants which set the pattern for Breton, a pattern maintained by the continuous transmarine intercourse up to the Middle Ages.

Two problems emerge from this. In the first place, it is still not clear why this migration took place. It must have been on a large scale. Here, it is worth recalling that between 1851 and 1891, Cornwall (which had then, as it has now, a population of about a third of a million) lost over 200,000 people through emigration, three-quarters of them to mining camps overseas. Studies of this movement make it clear that the first emigrants, often single men, attracted others at a time of economic depression by their tales of success, and that, when financially possible, the wives and families followed. A process along such lines might cautiously be argued in the Armorican movement, but the mainsprings were surely fears of hostile invasions. Whether these were all connected with the Anglo-Saxon advance westwards, spurred by notable English victories like that at Dyrham, Gloucestershire, in 577, is a matter of conjecture. It is conceivable that generally unsettled conditions at home, the (underestimated?) effects of the Irish colonies, and the lure of available land in Brittany, all have played their parts.

The second problem is archaeological. We can envisage a migration attaining five, if not six, figures – perhaps, over three centuries, up to a quarter- or half-million people (the population of England and Wales in Late Roman times could have been of the order of two to three million). It is most improbable that no material traces of this mass movement exist, and our ignorance here must be due to the fact that this post-Roman period is singularly poorly represented in French studies. As yet, only one clue has emerged. Dr Bernard Wailes has suggested that a particular type of pottery, found in post-Gallo-Roman contexts on a number of Breton sites – called *séricitique*, because the clay is gritted with talc (*séricite*) – may have been in use until the eleventh century AD. It occurs, too, in certain sites after the end of the Roman era, when reasons such as standing or partially standing buildings might have made them particularly attractive for immediate settlement. It cannot be derived from local Gallo-Roman wares, and Wailes argues that this fact, the contexts, and certain similarities in shapes, all imply that it is in fact the domestic pottery of the first immigrants, based on a known fifth- to sixth-century pottery style in west Cornwall ('Gwithian-style') which it resembles. There is room for much more work along these lines.

Our final puzzle concerns yet another migration, for which the evidence is admittedly incomplete. Galicia, the north-west part of Spain (the Roman *Gallaecia*), was occupied during the late fifth and sixth centuries by a Germanic people, the Suevi, who established an independent Christian kingdom in this region of granite hills and fierce coasts – not unlike Cornwall and Brittany. Among its various Christian sees, one of which, *Dumium*, was monastic rather than parochial, was a see described in 572 as *Britonensis ecclesia*, that of 'the church of the Britons'. It is now represented by Mondoñedo, some 40 miles north of Lugo. The bishop, in 572, was called *Mahiloc* or *Mailoc*, which is neither a Roman nor a Germanic name, but a Celtic one. In a sixth-century document describing the ecclesiastical organization of Galicia, there are references to 'the churches which are amongst the Britons' and also to 'the monastery of Maximus' in this see. The see stretched eastwards, across the river Eo, into the province of Asturias, and if this represents the sixth-century settlement, it involved a large stretch of coastal land. In the seventh century, there is a reference to *Britaniensis ecclesia*, and the present Santa María de Bretoña, at Pastorizo near Mondoñedo, perpetuates the name through a monastic foundation.

Were these 'Britons' from Britain, or from Brittany? We cannot be sure, but (as Edward Thompson remarks) to suppose that the fugitives from Britain had landed in Armorica before going on to Spain is merely to multiply hypotheses. The obvious and seemingly unusual monastic element in their church, the Celtic name, the continual use of the word *Brito*, all link this remarkable and little-known settlement with the homeland, if not with the homeland's Armorican offshoot as well; and it deserves to be recorded in this discussion.

Chapter Three

Christianity

The Irish, in this respect more practical than the British, call the period from the early fifth century to the late eighth 'Early Christian'. Not for them the obsolescent alternative of 'The Dark Ages', nor the slightly confusing 'Early Medieval' – for the latter can possess different meanings according to whether pure history or pure archaeology is in question. There is much to be said for extending 'Early Christian' to all of Britain, and the argument that several component peoples (the Picts, and nearly all Anglo-Saxons) were not in fact Christian until the seventh century loses its force if we consider such time-hallowed labels as 'Bronze Age' and 'Iron Age'. By no means everyone used objects of bronze or iron respectively throughout these prehistoric eras; the terms describe the periods commencing from the moment when either material began to be exploited, because such innovations at once offered a fresh potential for change in technology and thus in agriculture, warfare, trade, and even social structure. Christianity, from Roman to Viking times, was not just a religion that happened to survive. It was a code of ethics, a way of life, literature, education, the commemoration of the dead, a major import customer, a tenurial power, a social system, a patron of pure and applied arts, a missionary society, and so much else beside. As, in recent decades, a new generation of historians and archaeologists have been attracted to the study of early Christianity in Britain and Ireland, we know roughly twice as much about this subject as was known in 1940, and our knowledge goes on increasing all the time. We can examine, very concisely, the impact of this Mediterranean-born faith on the far north-west, bearing in mind the multiple nature of that impact.

The Church in Roman Britain

When did Christians first meet to worship in Roman Britain? We can safely claim that this happened in the third century, and despite the paucity of direct historical references it is not unlikely that it occurred in the second as well. Christianity was one of a number of religions – State-supported emperor-worship and the official Roman pantheon, Mithraism, some Eastern mystery-cults, localized devotion to Celtic godlings and to certain major deities – current in Britain. Its predominance by the end of the fourth century is not a specifically British trend; it reflects the universal rise of Christianity throughout the Empire.

In the latter centuries, the major landmarks were the periodical persecutions of Christians – in 202, in the 250s under Decius and Valerian, and again at the end of the century and the opening of the fourth. These provided Britain with her first martyrs; St Alban at Verulamium, either in the 250s or, as has now been argued by John Morris, as early as 209, and Aaron and Julian at Caerleon. From the reign of Constantine, proclaimed Emperor in Britain in 306, came first the grant of liberty of conscience to Christians, then in 311 Galerius' Edict of Toleration, and in March of 313 the so-called Edict of Milan, announcing a policy of complete religious tolerance, the restoration of sequestered churches, and full liberty of worship.

The precise nature of any Christian organization in Roman Britain, the identity of the Christian flocks, their distribution and extent, and the physical form of their churches, are matters we glimpse very darkly indeed. Was the typical fourth-century Roman Christian a Briton,

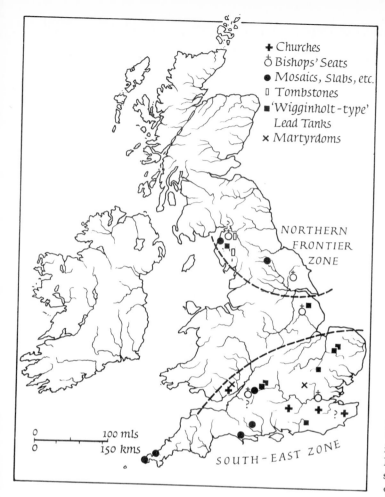

NORTHERN FRONTIER ZONE

SOUTH-EAST ZONE

0   100 mls
0   150 kms

51   The pattern of Christian evidences in late Roman Britain (omitting all small portable objects)

a Roman official, or an Eastern merchant? Was Christianity after Constantine mainly urban or mainly rural? Distribution-maps must be compiled with care. It is wise to exclude a growing catalogue of small portable objects bearing symbols or inscriptions of Christian character, since their find-spots may represent casual loss or theft. If we base such a map on Christian fixtures – 51 inscribed building-blocks, tombstones, villa mosaics, heavy lead baptismal tanks (if that is what they are), and 52 supposed church-sites – there is a distinct emphasis on south-east England, the most civilized, Romanized, and intensely populated area, with a secondary zone from York to the military frontier along and behind Hadrian's Wall. Should this surprise us? In detail, this map tells us little except that Christians were probably present in most major towns, and that (particularly in the south of England) there was a class of wealthy villa-owners who had Christian house-churches on their estates. In this *53, 54* latter group fall Lullingstone, Kent, with its remarkable *55* wall-paintings; and Hinton St Mary, Dorset, where the central roundel of a fourth-century mosaic gives us one of the Roman Empire's first portraits of Christ. We can note here that the Cross, best known of the Christian universal symbols, was still viewed with some ambiguity as the manner of Christ's death and as an emblem of criminal execution – it did not become widely current in Ireland or Britain much before 600 – and that in its place we find *56* the *chi-rho*, a monogram of the first two (Greek) capital letters in *Christos* ('the Anointed One – Christ').

The very existence of Christianity in fourth-century, and sub-Roman, Britain has long given rise to a related controversy; was Christianity over much of England expunged by the first Anglo-Saxon onslaughts from the mid-fifth century, and if so, does the fact that Christianity is found over so much of West and North Britain (in Cornwall, Wales, and northern England) in the fifth and sixth centuries simply mean that it was transferred thither by Christian refugees? It is possible that these have now become non-questions. We cannot be sure how widespread Christianity was in lowland England, nor that it was necessarily wiped out in all areas of English settlement – in Kent, for example, the reverse seems much more likely. In the west and north, Christian communities may well have been present in the fourth (if not third) centuries, even if we cannot yet show this; the growth of Christianity here in post-Roman times may be mainly indigenous or (more probably) fostered by prolonged

and intimate contact with the Church in Gaul and the Mediterranean. There are no special reasons for supposing that it owed anything to fellow-Christians migrating from the strife-torn south and east. Unhappily these questions, which embrace yet another issue, whether or not the Church in Celtic-speaking regions and in Ireland is directly in succession to the 'Roman', apostolic and papal church represented in fourth-century Roman Britain, have not always been free from sectarian and political ideas proper to much more recent centuries. One outcome of this confusion is the phrase 'the Celtic Church', which must be deplored if it carries any implication of original separatism. As Professor Jocelyn Toynbee has written, 'the so-called Celtic Church, surviving continuously in the west and north, was thoroughly Roman in creed and origin'. The only permissible label is 'the Church in Celtic-speaking Britain'.

Bishops and Dioceses

As Christianity grew and combined its isolated flocks, so it became necessary to provide some form of organization, which was loosely based on that of the Roman civil administration. Our own words 'diocese', 'rector', and 'vicar' share this ultimate source. The bishop,

53, 54 Among the earliest house churches in the West is the upper room complex in the Lullingstone, Kent, Roman villa. Painted wall plaster, *above*, shows the early (X plus P) form of chi-rho, in triumphal wreath and portico setting; this is the late C.D.E. Nicholson's painstaking reconstruction from plaster fragments found in the basement below the supposed chapel. *Below*, one of the six figures (portraits of members of the villa-owning family?) from the frieze on the west wall of the chapel or Upper Room. The *orans* posture – arms outstretched in prayer – is a common feature of early Christian art in Mediterranean lands

55, 56 *Above*, central roundel of the mosaic floor, from the main room of the Roman villa, Hinton St Mary, Dorset (now reassembled in the British Museum); late fourth century. Its chief importance lies in its recognition as probably the earliest representation of Christ in Britain – one of the earliest in the Western Empire. The objects either side of the head are pomegranates, symbols of Life Eternal. Other figure scenes on the pavement, though drawn from pagan mythology and literature, could be interpreted in terms of Christian allegory. In later centuries, the chi-rho, broken down into a compound of + and P, or merely + with a hooked top, appears on insular tombstones; that *below*, from St Just-in-Penwith (Cornwall), commemorates a late sixth-century person SELNIUS or SELINUS

episcopos or 'overseer', was at first little more than a local spiritual chairman. That a more complex state of affairs had evolved in fourth-century Britain is indicated by what we know of the Council of Arles in AD 314. Delegates from the civil diocese of Gaul included bishops from four of the five constituent civil provinces, in each case from the provincial capital. Now Roman Britain by 312 was organized into four such provinces, an extension of an earlier two (Britannia Superior, the south, and Inferior, the north).

Dr John Mann, discussing the list of delegates to this Council from Britain, has suggested that we are actually seeing our own provincial bishops for the first time. Bishop Eborius from York (capital of Britannia Secunda), Bishop Restitutus from London (Maxima Caesariensis), and Bishop Adelphius from – probably – Lincoln (for Flavia Caesariensis) are straightforward. 'Sacerdos presbyter' (another text quotes 'Sacer episcopus') and 'Arminius diaconus' are not located; John Mann suggests that they were from Britannia Prima, Wales and the West, with its probable capital at Corinium (Cirencester).

If this fascinating idea be true, there is no reason why this pattern of superior bishops should not be put further back, to the very late third century when the two provinces became four. Nor need these have been the *only* bishops, and by 314 one might suppose others to have been present in other towns from which we have evidence for Christian congregations. Its importance is that we see a fourth-century church organized in territorial dioceses, and this provides a basis for certain arguments as to the nature of British Christianity in sub-Roman times.

Ninian and Patrick

Ninian, a Roman Britain whose real name was 'Niniavus' or something very like it, first comes to our notice through Bede in the 720s. Bede was reporting a tradition

57

78

57 Link between two major Christian figures of seventh-century Northumbria; decorated initial from a twelfth-century MS. of Bede's Life of St Cuthbert, probably meant to show the Venerable Bede writing

which reached him from Whithorn, on the Galloway coast and 60 miles west of Carlisle. Galloway, part of a former native British state, had not long fallen to the Angles of Bede's Northumbria, and Northumbrian churchmen had assumed spiritual control, using what must have been the existing British episcopal seat at Whithorn for their own bishop, Pecthelm. The tradition, whose core need not be doubted, has clear Late Roman tones. Ninian was British, a reverend and holy bishop, regularly instructed in the Faith 'in Rome' (i.e. according to Roman Christian practice). His see was at Whithorn, 58, 59 where he was buried, and he built a stone church (i.e. in Roman fashion, as opposed to any native timberwork techniques) which was called *Candida Casa*, and gave its name to the place. Indeed this name in the original Latin or in a British equivalent must have survived to the eighth century, because Whithorn is simply the Northumbrian English translation (*hwít aern*, 'white house').

Apart from the improbability that this could all have taken place much after 400, Ninian's date is derived from (*a*) Bede's report that the see, or church, was in some fashion named after St Martin – Martin of Tours, who died in 397 or 398; and (*b*) less compellingly from later traditions about Ninian, from an eighth-century poem and from Ailred's medieval *Life*, which make Ninian the contemporary of some supposedly early fifth-century figures. Recent excavations deep below the crossing of

Whithorn Priory church, by P.R.Ritchie, have revealed at near-bedrock levels a group of inhumation burials. These are of Christian type, and appear to have disturbed some human cremations and a few sherds of colour-coated pottery (? Roman). One could read this as evidence for a settlement of Roman times, whose accompanying cemetery exhibits not only the third- to fourth-century shift of fashion from cremation to inhumation, but conceivably the advent of Christian ideas.

Why Whithorn, a remote burgh of no obvious geographical importance? There is quite a lot of evidence for semi-Romanized native life along the Dumfries and Galloway coastal belt, and life in this mild and sheltered region may have become increasingly attractive to the Britons of the various settlements along Hadrian's Wall, following Pictish attacks during the third and fourth centuries. Whithorn may have been a principal settlement. The advent of a bishop should mean, as Edward Thompson has stressed, not the establishment of some missionary outpost – there is no evidence for such an action at this period of Christianity – but that a group of Christians had asked to be given a bishop over them. Ninian may not even have been the first bishop. Whom would they ask? Here we revert to the supposed picture at the time of the Council of Arles, with British bishops from the four provinciae. Late in the fourth century, before the Theodosian attempts to restore the northern defences, a fifth province, Valentia, had been created. Arguments that Valentia was in Wales have less force than those which site it in the north or north-west, and the extensive walled settlement at Carlisle should have been its capital. There is good evidence for Late Roman Christianity in this area, and a fourth-century bishop at Carlisle can be postulated. To such a figure, the Christians of the Whithorn district, inconveniently far for immediate episcopal rule, would have made application for a bishop of their own.

58, 59 Physgyll cave, on the foreshore a few miles from Whithorn. *Below*, view of interior, showing grave-markers (beginning in the seventh century) against the wall; this secondary use as a burial-area was revealed during excavations. Whether or not Ninian actually used this cave for a retreat, an eighth-century poem of Whithorn origin does refer to the saint's withdrawal to some *horrendum antrum* ('an awesome cavern') that must surely be Physgyll

In line with this thinking are detailed arguments which suppose that, over the fifth and sixth centuries, southern Scotland between the two Walls was organized into several such dioceses. Whether Christianity ever attained more than local importance, hinted at by a group of inscribed memorial stones dated to these two centuries, we cannot say. A diocese based on Carlisle, with another at Whithorn, would have covered much of the native kingdom of Rheged; another on the southern shores of the Forth would have served the *Gododdin* (and the late sixth-century poem of the same name depicts a Christian ruling class in this area); a sixth-century diocese centred on what is now Glasgow and associated with St Kentigern (Mungo) would be proper to the British kingdom of Strathclyde; and in the Tweed Valley, notably around Peebles, there may have been a fourth, serving at least part of the British principality we know later as Bernicia. One can go a small step further, and argue that *Aebber-curnig* (Abercorn, west of Edinburgh) and *Mailros* (Old Melrose, on the Tweed,) were, like Whithorn, the diocesan seats of sub-Roman bishoprics; for, unlike the great majority of the later (Anglian) Northumbrian monasteries, these kept their British place names throughout.

In sub-Roman Wales and Cornwall, and those parts of England not soon overrun by Germanic settlers, the assumption must be that bishops and dioceses continued. In the absence of fixed Roman provincial divisions and (for the most part) urban centres, it is likely that the diocesan unit, as in southern Scotland, bore some relation to the native kingdom, if to any definite territory. Who for instance, were the seven British bishops who assembled about 600 to meet St Augustine from Canterbury – later tradition claimed (without much basis) at Aust-on-Severn? Were they the diocesan bishops from Dumnonia and the Welsh kingdoms?

St Patrick, like St Ninian, provides us with another case. We possess two works, now reliably restored, which can plausibly be regarded as Patrick's own writings; the *Confessio*, a partial autobiography written late in his life and intended to justify certain aspects of his career, and an *Epistola* directed against a native king – Coroticus, probably of Strathclyde – whose troops had reduced Christian converts to captivity. Patrick (Patricius) was his Roman name; his native British name may have been Sucatus (? 'good in battle'). Without venturing into lengthy argument, it can be stated briefly that Patrick was probably born in the late fourth century; was captured by Irish slave-raiders when he was a lad, and taken to Ireland. After some years as a slave, he escaped on a ship to the Continent. He eventually returned to Britain, having been trained in some ecclesiastical context, and, having been consecrated a bishop, went a second time to Ireland (this in 432) to minister to Christians there. He died in 461. Christianity may have reached (southern) Ireland in the fourth century from parts of western Britain, probably South Wales, and Pope Celestine in 431 (according to a Gaulish chronicle) had sent another Briton, Palladius, 'to the Irish believers in Christ, as their first bishop'. This short-lived mission, for some reason, failed; Patrick replaced him, surely under the direction of the British episcopate.

Where was Patrick's original home? He was from a Christian family, a landed family; his father was a decurion. His home was in a western region, exposed to Irish raiders; internal clues in his writing point north rather than south. The most attractive reading of the relevant place-name is as 'Banna Venta Berniae', where Bernia is a lost district name and Banna is some small centre (*venta*, perhaps 'market-town'). The only appropriate place is in north-west England, where Banna should be near the western end of Hadrian's Wall – possibly

Bewcastle. If this be so, we are back within any Late Roman and sub-Roman diocese of the Carlisle region, and Patrick's background is that of Ninian. One dares to imagine that the two men were contemporaries, or even schoolfellows.

Ireland was not, of course, converted universally overnight. We have no archaeology, and precious little history, of the Patrician Church in Ireland. But, as Dr Kathleen Hughes has shown, by the sixth century, Irish Christianity was under the rule of bishops. Each bishop held authority within his own *paruchia* (diocese); the *paruchia* was, in general, co-terminous with one or other form of Irish territorial division, probably the *tuath* – a petty kingdom, rather smaller than the post-Roman kingdoms of Britain.

In general, we see that ecclesiastical organization in both (non-Saxon) Britain and Ireland was, by the late fifth and early sixth centuries, a regular one, inherited from the Church of Late Roman times, and modified only in the light of native circumstances. Upon this pattern was to be imposed a very different one, that of the great monasteries.

The First Monasteries

Under the early persecutions, particularly in the Roman provinces of Egypt and the Near East, many Christians had fled into the desert. Some sought a solitary life, with extremes of physical hardship; others, a little later, came together in large or small groups for aspects of both worship and work. A definite philosophy, owing something to earlier ideas of spiritual progress, evolved around these ascetics; and by the troubled times of the fourth century, when the Christian Church, part of the Imperial establishment, was in the eyes of many of its members prey to certain worldly dangers, this Oriental monasticism attained high peaks of prestige. A stream of visitors from most parts of the Roman Empire went to see for themselves. Books, describing their visits, or detailing the lives of the more notable monastic founders, circulated widely and influentially. By the end of the fourth century, establishments in imitation of those in the Eastern deserts had sprung up – Lérins and Marseilles in the south of Gaul, Martin's further north at Ligugé and at Marmoutier near Tours.

If we seek to know when monasticism first reached Britain, we must be clear just what we understand by this term. Deliberate withdrawal from material affairs, with vows of chastity or poverty or continence, had long been practised by individuals. Patrick's writings allude to this in Ireland in his own day. It is quite possible that enlarged ideas on these lines were propagated in parts of fifth-century Britain. St Germanus of Auxerre (d. 448), whom Patrick may well have known in Gaul, as Ninian may conceivably have known the earlier St Martin of Tours – this is far less likely – visited Britain in 429 primarily to combat an intellectual heresy put about by a Briton, Pelagius. Germanus came again, soon after 400. But we have no evidence that monasticism, in the sense in which we see this in (say) seventh-century Ireland, was thus introduced. We look here to a distinct phenomenon; large bodies of monks, living in one fixed community, subject to an abbot and to a regular rule. This, with the ancillary aspects such as the provision of certain education, 'communal hermitages' (to be discussed again), and occasional extremes of ascetic existence, appears to reproduce a particular form of Oriental monasticism, the coenobitic or communal life already imitated' by St Honoratus' monastery on the island of Lérins and, in an idiosyncratic way, by St Martin of Tours.

The former difficulties inherent in imagining how this quite unfamiliar mode of Christian life could arrive, quite swiftly and without much apparent change from the east

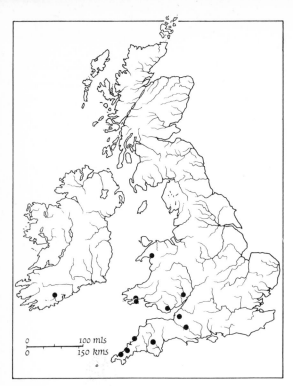

60 Distribution-map of finds of imported pottery. Class A: fine red wheel-made bowls and dishes from the Mediterranean ('Late Roman B and C', North Africa, Egypt and the Levant). Very late fifth and sixth centuries AD

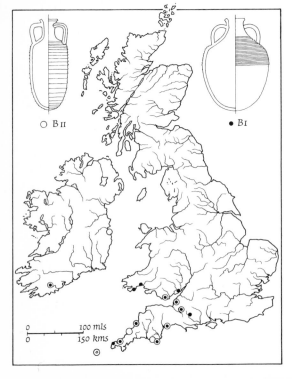

61 Distribution-map of imported amphorae of Classes B i and B ii. B i, so-called 'combed amphorae', and B ii, a ribbed type, appear to come from the Aegean and Asia Minor. Mostly sixth and early seventh centuries AD

62 *Right*, Aerial view of Tintagel, north Cornwall. A monastery flourished here between the late fifth and eighth centuries AD

Mediterranean model, along the further shores of western Britain have now been largely resolved. Archaeological work has shown that certain types of wheel-made pottery, clearly non-British, which have been found at post-Roman sites in a number of areas of Ireland, Wales, and the south-west, are direct imports from the Mediterranean. Some are table-wares in the former Samian and Arretine tradition, unusual in having Christian symbols stamped on them; others, containers for wine (eucharistic wine?) or perhaps oil. Sources must include many of the major Eastern ports, like Antioch, Tarsus, Athens, and Constantinople, and (for at least some of the table-wares) North Africa, while the wine itself may have come from Rhodes or Chios. Thanks largely to the labours of Dr John Hayes, much of this material is approximately dated – more closely in many cases than similar wares current in Roman Britain.

60, 61

63 Ornamental initials appear in Insular MSS. during the later sixth century. The *Cathach* of St Columba is a psalter, probably late sixth century, conceivably penned by Columba himself

This trade is a widespread Eastern one, and sherds found on Irish or Cornish sites may and do possess exact counterparts unearthed in the Crimea, far up the Danube, in Cyrenaica, and even along the Nile to places in Ethiopia. The western Mediterranean is scarcely involved at all. Direct sea-trade, through the Straits of Gibraltar to the west of Britain, is now almost certain. Where such platters and amphorae could travel, so too could pilgrims to and from the Holy Land, occasional refugees, books, and ideas. There is much in all this that we do not, and may never, really understand; but on present showing the earliest dateable monastery, in the sense of a true Insular counterpart of a Mediterranean model, would be

62 Tintagel, on the north Cornish coast, during the period AD 470 to 500. 'Tintagel' is a Norman-French name for the later castle on the same site, and its British name may have been Rosnant, 'the promontory by the valley', which suits its topography.

The rapid spread of monastic ideas over the next half-century has yet to be worked out in detail. The south coast of Wales, with early monasteries at Lantwit Major (Llanilltud Fawr – the *first* Llanilltud may, as Hugh

64 The summit of Christian art in stone; the great High Crosses, panelled with biblical scenes. Muiredach's Cross, Monasterboice, Co. Louth; the east face (early tenth century)

65 Stylized figure of a bishop with bell and crozier; stone pillar from White Island, Lough Erne, Co. Fermanagh, one of a group of archaic-looking sculptures, probably of the ninth century

Williams thought, have been Caldy Island), Nantcarban or Llancarfan, and Llandaff in Cardiff, inspired others: St David's, in the kingdom of Dyfed, Llanbadarn on the Cardiganshire coast, Bangor in the north-west. King Maelgwn is said to have given the remains of the Roman shore-fort at Holyhead to St Cwbi to found a monastery in the next century (Caergwbi).

64-7   By the early sixth century, a couple of generations after Patrick's death, monasticism had reached central and southern Ireland; partly perhaps through the same sea-trade, which touched both the Cork shore and Dublin Bay, but mostly through the agency of contact with Wales. From the middle of the century to its end, most of the great monastic foundations arose, many of them associated with the traditional pupils of St Finnian of Clonard, of whom St Ciarán (of Clonmacnois) and St
63   Columba or Columcille, an aristocrat from the north, are the best known.

66 The most famous portable reliquary or 'house-shaped shrine'; the Monymusk Reliquary or *Brecbennoch* (Edinburgh). Of late seventh- or early eighth-century date, and perhaps Scottish origin, it is only 105 mm across, with gilt and silver ornaments on wood, and may have housed a relic of St Columba

67 The Athlone Crucifixion, an openwork bronze plaque which would be riveted to a (wooden) book-cover. This eighth-century Irish object shows Christ crucified, with attendant angels, lance-bearer and sponge-profferer, all figures being stylized; compare the Calf of Man Crucifixion of the same period (*ill.* 43)

Nor did the impetus stop here. In 563, Columba sailed to the Irish colony in Argyll, to found the monastery of Iona. Lesser-known Irishmen – St Moluoc of Lismore, and later, St Maelrubha of Applecross in Wester Ross – followed this example. Possibly in the late sixth, or early seventh century, Whithorn itself became, under Irish influence, the monastic establishment that the Northumbrians encountered around 700. Maughold, in the Isle of Mann, is another instance. Irish monks and clerics, voyaging up the west coast, reached Orkney, where such monasteries as Birsay and Deerness may belong to the early seventh century; and Shetland, with slightly later monasteries like Papil.

In 634–35, an accident of history – the fact that a Northumbrian prince, Oswald, had been exiled among the Dalriadic Scots where he received a Christian education and learnt the Irish language – brought Aidan of Iona to Northumbria. On Lindisfarne or Holy Isle, Aidan and

68 The Rupertus Cross (now in Bischofshofen church, near Salzburg).
Just over 5 feet high, it is possibly an English product of the early ninth
century, and a rare survivor of a once-widespread type of ornament

his brethren to some extent reproduced the conditions of
Iona. The story of the other great Northumbrian monasteries – Old Melrose, Coludesburh (St Abb's Head,
Berwickshire), Abercorn, Whitby, Jarrow and Monkwearmouth, to name only some – comes down to us from
Bede: and from him, and other sources, we see the spread
of monasticism to the newly converted English kingdoms, Mercia, East Anglia, and Wessex. Both Irish and
68 English monks, by this time true missionaries, went
further, eager to convert the still pagan peoples of the
Germanic homelands, Frisia, the Low Countries, and the
various territories of Germany. Irish monastic foundations, many of them today in existence as famous names,
stretched across the Alps, through Switzerland to Italy,
and thus back to the Mediterranean again; here, in the
guise of such foundations as St Benedict's on Monte
Cassino, the long thread of Insular monasticism met its
sister-branches.

It is a massive and inspiring story, one of the strangest
aspects of Christianity in western Europe. The impact of
monasticism on Irish society would alone fill a substantial
book. Physically, an early Irish or British monastery was
unusual. An enclosure, the monastic *vallum*, was generally
required. A very few of the earliest – Iona, Clonmacnois,
possibly Glastonbury if (as many think) there was a late-
fifth-century foundation there – are within extensive
enclosures, defined by major earthworks, of rectangular
rather than curvilinear form. This may recall the Eastern
deserts, where all fortifications are normally rectangular
and where, by the fifth and sixth centuries, monasteries
were frequently so protected from marauders. The majority of Insular monasteries were sited within abandoned
hill-forts, or (as with Tintagel, Deerness, Coludesburh,
and Old Melrose) in coastal or inland promontory-forts,
protected by a bank and ditch across the neck, or even in
deserted Saxon shore-forts; Bede lists several examples of

69 The Great Skellig rock, off the coast of south-west Ireland

this. Later monasteries were obliged to provide their own enclosures, generally of round or oval lay-out.

Nor was the ascetic element forgotten. In the Celtic world, as in the hotter Levant, solitary spiritual contest ranked very high, and many that we should now regard as eccentric or extreme were seen clearly to be persons of some special gift. As well as the more familiar hermit, common at most stages and in most areas of Christianity, we find small and isolated monasteries – notably on islands – which we can only call 'communal hermitages' or perhaps 'eremitic monasteries'. The classic site is that of Sceilg Mhichíl, on the vast natural pyramid of the Great Skellig rock, one of a group some miles off the Co. Kerry coast. The Outer Hebrides and the Northern Isles provide other examples.

69, 70

70 Aerial view of Sceilg Mhichil, showing the ledge-like enclosures and the scarcely distinguishable corbelled stone oratories and living-cells

St Augustine at Canterbury

In the sixth century, Kent – Jutish and Frankish rather than Saxon – was the most civilized area of the English settlement, and the one in which a high degree of continuity from Roman and sub-Roman times may be postulated. Pope Gregory (the Great), traditionally inspired by the sight of pagan English slaves at Rome, was moved to attempt the conversion of the English. Ethelbert, king of Kent and at this stage the dominant English monarch, permitted Gregory's emissary, Bishop Augustine, to land with his companions at Thanet (597). Ethelbert's wife Bertha was a Christian Frankish princess – the Frankish language was very close to the Old English dialects, and the interpreters whom Augustine brought with him were, Bede says, drawn from among (Continental) Franks.

Ethelbert's reception of this Mediterranean mission, if Bede's Canterbury-derived report of his welcoming speech is realistic, was peculiarly tolerant and urbane. He permitted them to use St Martin's church at Canterbury, which Bede says had been built during (Late) Roman times – this is arguable, but not impossible – and Ethelbert himself, with his circle, were duly converted.

Augustine's correspondence with Gregory, giving reports of progress and seeking advice, is preserved for us by Bede. Doubts have been cast on the genuineness of these letters, but the overall tone and subject-matter surely represents the gist of a real interchange. They contain much of great interest. Gregory, for example, excluding Gaulish bishops from Augustine's charge, none the less gave him complete authority – an authority he was unable to exercise – over 'all the bishops of Britain'. In 601, a letter whose provisions repay study was received. Sending to Augustine the *pallium*, mark of promotion to what we would today call an archbishop, and dispatching a fresh party of senior churchmen to help him, Gregory lays down the lines on which Church government in Britain is to be organized. Canterbury, centre of the Kentish kingdom, is chosen as the archiepiscopal throne. Augustine is to consecrate twelve other bishops within the ecclesiastical province of Canterbury. A suitable bishop is to be found for York, who is to consecrate a further twelve bishops of his own, forming a northern province under himself as metropolitan. London is to have its own metropolitan, a separate see and synod. Canterbury is to remain permanently superior to both London and York.

This scheme, which largely describes the present Church of England, carries endless implications. Gregory,

71

71 Large gold *solidus* with self-portrait, coined at York by Archbishop Wigmund (837–854); an extraordinary, Mediterranean-inspired token of the importance of the northern see

72 The pectoral cross (span, 60 mm) of St Cuthbert, as a bishop. In gold cloisonné and filigree set with garnets, this is Northumbrian workmanship of the mid-seventh century

73 St Dunstan, the Somerset-born ecclesiastical reformer, abbot of Glastonbury (from 945) and archbishop of Canterbury (960–988), abases himself at Christ's feet; detail from a tenth-century MS

essentially a religious diplomat from a wholly urban Roman Church, sees Britain in terms of a network of 72, 73 urban episcopacies, like the civilized world with which he is familiar. But only London, surviving in some mercantile fashion, and the remains of Roman York, about this time the seat of the Northumbrian kingdom, really comply with his ideas outside the kingdom of Kent. Excluding London, what were the 26 cities in mind? Is this based on some aspect of sub-Roman Britain? What connection, if any, is there with a list of 28 cities in Britain preserved in the collection of documents edited by Nennius in the early ninth century, a list which includes both Roman towns and *civitas* capitals?

In so far as Kent was concerned, Augustine was able to consecrate (604) bishops of London and Rochester. Ethelbert's successors were less well disposed to Christianity, and there were setbacks. In 625, Paulinus was consecrated bishop of York, and sent to Northumbria, where King Edwin, shortly to be converted, had arranged to marry Ethelbert of Kent's daughter. This was followed (627) by a Northumbrian rejection of heathenism, and the equivalent of national baptism ('all the nobility and a large number of humbler folk', Bede tells us) in the river Glen, by one of the royal palaces, Yeavering in Northumberland. Edwin, in his turn the dominant English ruler, was in part responsible for the conversion in the same year of the East Anglians, and Paulinus, who was in 634 raised to metropolitan status, began work in Lindsey (roughly the modern Lincoln).

It is probable that, had fate not intervened, all the early English kingdoms would by the mid-seventh century have been converted, under the aegis of Canterbury and York. But, late in 633, Mercia, the great pagan kingdom of central England, fought against Northumbria, and Edwin was slain; Paulinus and the Christian queen fled, and when, two years later, Northumbria was again ascendant, it was under the Bernician Oswald. Oswald looked not south but north-west for the spiritual pastors of his united realm. He looked to Iona, bishop Aidan, and the by now mainly monastic Church of Ireland and the Irish colonies. There had been, in the recent turmoils, great backslidings among the swiftly converted Northumbrian people, whose acquaintance with Christianity through Paulinus' efforts cannot have been deep-rooted. Seventh-century Northumbria was to become a mighty Christian province, but of a particular flavour.

Northumbria's Golden Age

At certain phases of Insular history, the right men seem to have existed in the right places at the right time. Northumbria – Northumberland and Durham, with extensions north, south, and west – in the century from about 640 is an example. The Angles of Northumbria, in origin a small armed settlement under their leader Ida on the harsh north-eastern shore, with their citadel of Bamburgh, are to the percipient historian a people with marked and notable characteristics, sufficient indeed to raise doubts as to whether the portmanteau term 'Anglo-Saxon' possesses any real validity. If landscapes can mould peoples, the northern hills and valleys and wild grey coasts left their mark on the early Northumbrians just as the industrial fields of this area have shaped their modern descendants.

We are fortunate in that some of our best sources – a group of religious *Lives*, all produced in Northumbrian monasteries, and above all Bede's great *History*, one of the supreme personal monuments in European literature – come from late seventh-century and early eighth-century Northumbria. They depict a vigorous expanding kingdom, in which, despite the predominance of Old English speech, it is hard not to see a considerable Anglian fusion with the northern British. From the religious viewpoint,

74 Insular manuscript illumination; a 'carpet page' from the Lindisfarne
Gospels. In this staggering achievement, created *c.* 698 by a Northumbrian,
we see the counterpart of the finest decorative metalwork (*cf. ill.* 102)

75　In contrast to the Hiberno-Northumbrian idiom of *ill.* 74, this page from the Benedictional of St Aethelwold is part of the European tradition; it exemplifies the tenth-century 'Winchester School' in southern Britain

76 The nave of Brixworth church (Northants), looking west. A great basilican church of the late seventh century

76

there was a long and interesting conflict of styles. Monasteries, particularly the northern ones, and any founded before the 660s, conform in character and (as far as archaeology can show us) in physical type to the general pattern over West and North Britain. The ancillary field-monuments – enclosed developed cemeteries, shrines, internal monastic features – are, for half a century, in the same mould. Yet Northumbria looked east, across the seas to the Continent, and to a lesser extent south to other Christian areas. Bede, whose canonical disapproval of any ecclesiastical system ruled by monastic houses instead of diocesan bishops is clear enough, was forced to comment on this aspect at Iona and Lindisfarne, despite his admiration and affection for the saintly Aidan. In a famous synod held at Whitby in 664, the Northumbrian royal

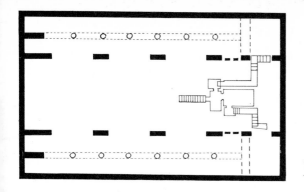

77, 78 *Above*, simplified plan of another famous basilica, Hexham Abbey, built 672–678 by Bishop Wilfrid of Ripon. The little separate eastern chapel now lies below the choir; the relic-crypt is also Wilfrid's work. *Below*, the Hexham 'Frith Stool', a seventh-century monolithic throne for an abbot, imitating a Byzantine model

house and Christian dignitaries could no longer avoid the clear choice; was their kingdom to continue on the lines of the monastic churches in Ireland and outlying Britain, or was it to fall in line with Canterbury, Europe, and Rome? The decision went to the latter course; it was in some respects painful, but it was inevitable. Monasteries like the double foundation of Jarrow and Monkwearmouth, Bede's home, and great churches at Hexham and Ripon followed. Not only the tenor of Christian government but the necessary art, architecture, and scholarship all draw on native Christian roots, but they also look outwards to the Church in Gaul and to European Christianity.

77, 78

74, 75

The wealth and importance of the Church in national life, the prestige of individual Northumbrian churchmen,

79–81 *Left*, an Evangelist's symbol, the Lion of St Mark, from the so-called Echternach Gospels, whose script, of Irish origin, has certain English characteristics. This book may have been taken from Northumbria to the Continent by St Willibrord (658–739), or else have been written at Echternach (now in Luxembourg), where Willibrord established a monastery soon after 700. Slightly more 'primitive' is the St Matthew page, *right*, from the Book of Durrow, the figure distinctly reminiscent of metalwork. In contrast, the St John, *far right*, from the Book of Kells is solemnly enthroned in a naturalistic setting

and the rise of learning, were reflected in a notable world of artistic accomplishment. From the northern scriptoria, particularly at Lindisfarne where the Irish and Germanic art-traditions could be blended with innovations from the Mediterranean and classical school, came some of the 79–81 outstanding illuminated gospel-books of any age. The *Lindisfarne Gospels*, the *St Chad* and the *Echternach Gospels*, and the slightly later *Codex Amiatinus*, produced at Jarrow-Monkwearmouth in the early eighth century and designed to be a gift for the Pope, would alone justify the title of 'the Golden Age'. They continue, particularly in the case of the first three, a slightly earlier tradition seen in the *Book of Durrow* (670s; Irish, or Irish–Northumbrian) and maintained in the great *Book of Kells* (which is later, probably begun at Iona in the very late eighth century, and because of Norse raids finished in Ireland at the start of the ninth). The interchange of motifs, emphases,

and art-styles among all the differing media – manuscripts, fine metalwork, carved stone, even bone, leather, and wood – is an aspect of Insular art at this period which requires a book to itself, and we can only note one aspect here; the Pictish debt to Northumbria. From the second quarter of the eighth century, Pictish art, hitherto generally confined to stone and a little metalwork and relying mostly upon the native 'animal style', takes on fresh elaborations which point to Northumbrian, rather than to Irish, borrowings.

The Christian Dead

The specialized archaeology of early Christianity in Britain and Ireland is a topic of quite recent growth, and preliminary studies – coupled with selective excavation – show that we stand to learn a very great deal in this way. One solitary matter may be examined now, the treatment of the Christian dead.

82, 83 Fifth-century rustic tombstones in a decaying Roman idiom; *above*, of CUNAIDE, from Hayle, west Cornwall, and *below*, of LATINUS and his little daughter, from Whithorn

Christians were normally buried lying full length and without grave-goods; among the Germanic peoples, to whom grave-goods were clearly of much importance, objects were in fact often deposited in graves for some time after conversion. The grave lies east–west, head to the west, and can reflect pre-Christian fashions; simple dug-graves, graves in long stone cists, rock-cut graves, graves with wooden coffins or timber linings. One suspects that many graves were marked, if only by small sticks or stones; it is not easy otherwise to account for the common discovery of regular parallel rows.

A limited number of graves were properly commemorated. This custom stems from both Roman Britain and European Christian practice, and stone slabs or pillars bearing the name of the deceased and other details, *82–84* incised in Latin capital letters, occur in North Britain, Wales, and the south-west, from the fifth to eighth centuries. The forms of wording, the inscribed memorial formulae, show distinct affinities with Gaulish and Mediterranean models, and must be connected with the sea-borne nexus discussed in the context of monastic ideas. In southern Ireland, a different alphabet – ogam, using not letters but groups of long and short strokes across a base-line – appears to have been invented in Late Roman times through southern Irish/South Welsh contact. The earliest Irish ogam-inscribed stones may not in fact be Christian at all, though after the fifth century the majority must be. Ogam-inscribed stones are found in Irish-settled areas in Wales and Cornwall, often bilingual – they repeat the name of the dead man and his father, or tribe, in Latin letters – and we also have normal Latin inscriptions giving us distinctively Irish names. In the same areas, Latin inscriptions reading vertically, not horizontally, and including the deceased's father's name, are sixth- and seventh-century modifications under Irish influence.

84 A Latin inscription, probably commemorating the founder of the church and his wife – *Hic bea(tu)s Saturninus se(pultus) (j)acit et sua sa(ncta) (?) conju(n)x*. Llansadwrn Church, Anglesey, sixth century

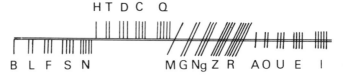

The 'H' Surface   H T D C Q

The 'B' Surface   B L F S N   M G Ng Z R A O U E I

85, 86 The Ogam alphabet – short and long strokes, above, below, across and through the line – with an instance (the tomb of MAQI-LIAG son of ERCA) from Co. Kerry and a sixth-century bilingual tombstone from Cornwall; the ogam reads INGENAVI MEMOR

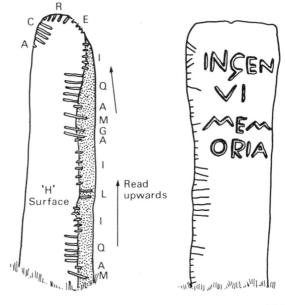

87 Church Island, Co. Kerry. Reconstrucion of enclosed developed cemetery, oratory, living-cell and circular wall around burial-area (eighth century)

The Picts, as we saw earlier, may also have adopted the habit of erecting monuments, their Class I stones, from an acquaintance with Roman models. Much more simple is a great group of small cross-inscribed stones (slabs or pillars), the smallest of which are really cross-inscribed grave-markers – plaques or pebbles placed directly on, sometimes even in, the grave. The crosses are 'primary' – simple linear forms, sometimes combined with circles and minor embellishments. These date from about 600, and are commoner in the north (northern Ireland, north-west Wales, Mann, western Scotland, and the Isles), the custom being diffused through the Church in Ireland. The impetus here possibly comes from tiny initial crosses in manuscripts, even from cross-marked objects in Christian use, and occasionally names are added to these cross-marked stones; conversely, small initial or heading crosses can be added to ogam- or Latin-inscribed stones in the southern provinces.

The various regional schools of large and high stone crosses – in south-west Scotland, Ireland, Wales, and Cornwall – are not only in the main non-commemorative of the dead, but fall outside our period; as do the bulk of the 'recumbent slabs' of Ireland and the Irish colonies, an

aggrandized and later version of some aspects of the earlier grave-markers.

Cemeteries – consecrated areas set specially apart for the Christian dead – assume special importance because they, not the almost unknown churches, are the first field-monuments of Insular Christianity. Roman pagan, and Christian, and presumably sub-Roman Christian, cemeteries were outside settlements, often by roads, and not necessarily enclosed; very large 'open' cemeteries of this kind, with hundreds if not thousands of graves, were used in the fifth and sixth centuries, notably in southern Scotland and parts of the south-west. Yet alongside these, as an aspect of the general British reassertion, we find much smaller enclosed cemeteries, burial-grounds for neighbourhoods and families rather than for continuing urban settlements or tribal districts. These smaller cemeteries are enclosed, the enclosure taking the form of a circular or oval or curvilinear bank (bank and ditch, wall). This is a British and Irish speciality, and appears to owe much to an almost immemorial tradition of the circular sacred plot – one seen successively in henge monuments, causewayed camps, barrows and ring-ditches, cremation cemeteries, aspects of Romano-Celtic

88 Moyne Grave-yard, small monastic enclosure near Shrule, Co. Mayo; note the burial-area and traces of internal divisions

87–9

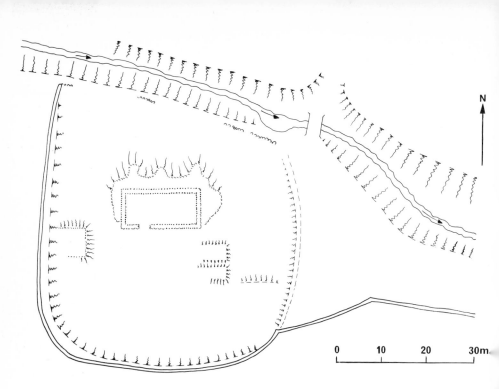

89　Enclosed developed cemetery at Kirkmaiden (Old Kirk), Rinns of Galloway. The church-foundations (centre) represent some medieval replacement

90　The Glamis Manse stone (*cf. ill.* 30); the reverse face, with a Pictish Class II decorated relief cross, symbols and figure-scene. Eighth century

temples and mausolea, and (in lowland England) perhaps influenced by uncommon Roman walled cemeteries and burial-plots.

In the seventh and eighth centuries, the enclosed cemetery (which, throughout Ireland and most of West and North Britain, was probably the only visible focus of Christianity in any given area) becomes 'developed'; that is, enriched by the addition of a small chapel, often at first of timber, by 700 and later increasingly often in stone. In the monastic church, individual brethren, combining what we might regard as sporadic mission-work, spiritual retreat, and a rudimentary pastoral cure, may have resided in such developed cemeteries, as the addition of living-cells shows. Such holy men might, on death, be accorded distinctive graves, whose surrounds and above-ground elements reveal various traditions; those of the Mediterranean cult of Christian martyrs (rectilinear stone surrounds, the *cellae* of the early Church, or some form of altar-like superstructure), or else, like the cemetery-enclosure, features ultimately recalling Insular pre-Christian practices – small circular or recti-linear ditches around the grave. In many parts of Britain, particularly in south and west Scotland, Cornwall, to a lesser extent in Wales, and (this is not always recognized) in Northumbria too, the sites selected in the full Middle Ages to serve as parish churches have, despite successive rebuildings, clearly detectable origins in the enclosed developed cemeteries of pre-Norse times. Traces of a circular churchyard, internally raised by generations of burials and rewalled at intervals; surviving dedications in honour of obscure or localized saints; Early Christian cross-marked slabs or inscribed stones, found in bygone days and now preserved within the church; these are all the necessary clues, and in no respect is the past more notably part of the present than in this way.

91 Mary Magdalene washes Christ's feet; detail from the Ruth-well (Dumfriesshire) Cross, an isolated masterpiece (*c.* 700?)

90, 91

Chapter Four

Home and Hearth

It is fair to say that the archaeology of most of Britain and Ireland from the fifth to eighth centuries AD is known in outline (if not everywhere in equal detail) but, apart from several full studies of the early Anglo-Saxon settlements, it has not been discussed in one single volume. Such a book would be a very lengthy one, and only certain points of interest – with an emphasis on the unfamiliar – will be treated here.

Fortress and Citadel

Hill forts, British and Irish, occur in all shapes and sizes, and – if we stretch the term to include fortified hillocks, inland spurs, and coastal promontories – must be numbered in thousands. This particular mode of securing men's homesteads (temporarily or permanently) goes back to the start of the Early Iron Age – about the sixth century BC – and, outside the comparative civilization of the Roman provinces in Britain, hill-forts were still being occupied and constructed during the first centuries AD.

Of special interest is the fact that, even within Roman Britain, there is now much to suggest that perhaps by the end of the fourth century, and certainly during the fifth and sixth, fairly substantial hill-forts which had been unoccupied since the Roman conquest were once again selected as the equivalent of tribal capitals. In some areas the refurbishing amounted to the creation of new styles of fortification. Many reasons underlie this event. The Celts have never been, at any stage of their history, natural town-dwellers; unlike the Romans and other

Mediterranean-derived cultures, they lacked that millennia-long background of urban civilization. In Ireland, for instance, all the cities and most of the towns of any size owe their form, often their location and very existence, to Germanic initiative; to Vikings, Normans, or later English and lowland Scots settlers.

In sub-Roman Britain, as we have seen, scattered urban life based on fortuitously selected Roman walled towns did continue, in some cases unbroken to the present time. In the north and west, with the possible exceptions of Carlisle and one or two Welsh towns, the reversion to a non-Roman way of life in the native states did not involve urban capitals. It is questionable whether some of these principalities – Dumnonia is a safe example – ever possessed permanent capitals at all. If the constant references in the early Lives of Saints be taken as any sort of guide here, hill-forts, though deserted for centuries, were regarded as in some way the direct properties of native rulers; and hill-forts were chosen as their new seats. Apart from the desirable protection thereby afforded. such fortresses must have commanded much prestige; and even if we suppose, as with the historical Arthur, that the military presence occasionally took the shape of mobile cavalry bands, John Morris reminds us that such units in particular would require fortified bases during their most vulnerable times – periods of rest, and at night.

In the north, hill-forts and smaller citadels were in widespread use. The Picts in the sixth century were ruled by Bridei from one near Inverness – perhaps Craig Phadraig. Clatchard's Craig in Fife, now destroyed by quarrying, seems to have been another, and excavations produced fifth or sixth-century pottery and traces of some kind of large internal hall. Dundurn in Perthshire, under siege in the year 683, Dumyat near Stirling, and Denork in Fife are other elaborate hill-citadels which may have been used by Picts at this period.

92

92   Tap o'Noth, Aberdeenshire; a large vitrified fort, representative of the earliest Scottish hill-forts, some re-occupied centuries later

The Irish settlers in the west, the Dalriadic Scotti, were not only strangers in the land; they came from a country where rulers dwelled in forts. Citadels characterized this Argyll colony for centuries, Dunadd on the Moss of Crinan being the best known. Dunadd, like certain Pictish fortresses, is 'nucleated' – that is, the central citadel is surrounded by a series of irregular outworks. The same concept is found again in the lands of the northern British, south of the Forth–Clyde line, where post-Roman forts are commonplace. Dalmahoy, west of Edinburgh,

is nucleated; it may be that Dumbarton Rock on the Clyde, 'the *dún* of the Britons', began with this plan too. The present prominent rocks of both Stirling and Edinburgh Castle – the latter, certainly – housed post-Roman fortresses, and one could argue this in the case of Traprain Law in East Lothian (which may have been the home base of Cunedda and the *Gododdin* before the migration to north-west Wales), and also for the high spur of Durham Castle and Cathedral. One can note that the invading Angles in the sixth century made their first bridgehead on the rock of Bamburgh Castle, but only extensive excavation would show whether or not this was captured from a contemporary possessor.

Glimpses of minor forts are afforded from Galloway, south-west Scotland. A tiny one at Dunragit in Wigtown may indeed contain the name of *Reget* (Rheged), if that post-Roman kingdom, generally located with its centre in the Carlisle region, extended so far. Mote of Mark, near the Kirkcudbright shore, was both occupied and re-fashioned in the post-Roman era, and housed some metal-

93 Dumbarton Rock ('Stronghold of the Britons') in the Clyde; royal citadel of Strathclyde, probably fifth century AD

94

94 Traprain Law, east of Edinburgh, an ancestral fortress of the Votadini and perhaps Cunedda's family seat in late Roman times

working craftsmen who left their numerous little clay moulds there. Trusty's Hill, further west, seems to have been attacked and burnt, and a Pictish raiding-party in the sixth or seventh century must have done this; for, on a flat outcrop by its entrance, they carved certain symbols which commemorate the death of their own leader in this engagement.

In Wales, where the native (secular) literature makes it clear that hill-forts were generally used by rulers, there have been recent excavations. Degannwy, Dinorben (in Denbigh, for the start of sub-Roman times), and Dinas Emrys, where the last word, the Welsh for *Ambrosius*, recalls the fifth-century leader of that name, are three instances from North Wales; both Degannwy and Dinas Emrys have produced imported post-Roman pottery. Dinas Powys near Cardiff, very fully examined, is a smaller fort, appropriate to a *regulus*, or chieftain, which yielded numerous finds of fifth- to seventh-century date. Certain large hill-forts on the Welsh Marches, especially in the north, have also produced sherds of astonishingly coarse handmade pottery, with occasional evidence of small-scale rebuilding, and it has been suggested that these represent temporary bases for the incoming *Gododdin* or latter-day *Votadini* from south-east Scotland.

95   In Cornwall, only one Iron Age fort – Castle Dore, near Fowey, excavated before 1939 – can be claimed as a Dumnonian ruler's seat; it contained the remains of post-holes of a great timber hall, of the order of 40 × 80 ft., and this may have been used by an early sixth-century king, Cunomori ('Hound of the Sea'). The inscribed memorial stone of his son, Drustanus, still stands close by. Chun Castle, an imposing stone-walled citadel of the third century BC in the Lands' End, was reoccupied in the sixth century AD by persons using grass-marked pottery – presumably Irish settlers. Place-names suggest similar use of other small but prominent Cornish forts, like Dinmelioc

in the china-clay district of mid-Cornwall, now the parish churchyard of St Dennis.

Eastwards, there is very clear evidence of other Dumnonian post-Roman fortresses. Congresbury, near the Bristol Channel shore, between Weston and Bristol, is currently being excavated, and has already given us a mass of post-Roman pottery. On the south Devon coast, High Peak (Sidmouth) is an extraordinary little site, where the re-use (about AD 500) is stratified above a Neolithic occupation! Similar post-Roman wares have come from Glastonbury Tor, high above the Abbey, a very small and lofty eyrie. South Cadbury, a massive Iron Age hill-fort by the Somerset–Wiltshire border, has on the strength of a post-medieval folk-tale been claimed as 'Camelot', the seat of the 'King Arthur' of medieval fiction; its post-Roman use certainly involved, not only very sizeable buildings, but virtual refortification of the entire hill-top. Still further east, and beyond Dumnonia, one thinks of the mysterious 'Vespasian's Camp', a large oval hill-fort in a wood just west of Amesbury: for the first element in the name 'Amesbury' is again the Emrys, or Ambrosius, that suggests 'Ambrosius Aurelianus', last of the Romans and the forerunner of the historic Arthur.

95 Castle Dore, Cornwall; an Iron Age fortress, containing a sixth-century AD great timber hall, probably that of 'King Mark' (Marcus Cunomori)

The Lesser Dwellings

Domestic architecture in Britain and Ireland of post-Roman times exhibits at least three strains. In those parts scarcely touched, or not touched at all, by the Roman occupation, we can suppose that types of dwelling favoured in the Early Iron Age and during the centuries contemporary with Roman Britain continued to appear, subject to whatever strains of typological evolution we think we can detect. In areas which were Romanized, we cannot ignore the fact that plans and techniques – rectilinear rather than circular layout, improved methods of timber-framing, roofings other than mere thatch – must have left their mark and must have inspired imitations; to this we should add the influence of Christian architecture, since all known churches and chapels in Early Christian Ireland and post-Roman Britain are of rectangular plan. Finally, as in prehistory, regions devoid of handy free-stone will exhibit a preference for timber or wattle building, while highland regions with ample stone and comparatively little timber will show appropriately opposite preferences. This is not an immutable rule and there are known exceptions, but materials can of course influence both plans and dimensions – it is simply not possible to span, in rough stone masonry, rooms of the width that can be spanned in all-wooden constructions. The essentially timber-based nature of early Anglo-Saxon architecture (save for, from an intermediate stage, many churches) is not entirely due to ancestral skills in timberwork; it results from the nature of the resources and materials available in the relevant settlement-areas of lowland England.

In prehistory, Britain and Ireland constituted 'a roundhouse province' – that is, one where the commonest plan for a single-family dwelling was circular, a low stone (or turf, or composite) wall, with a radial thatched roof of depressed wigwam form. The word which underlies the usual term for 'house' in this sense in all the Celtic languages, *tigos*, seems to imply 'roof'; the house is distinctive in being the only circular stone construction, in a very large range of such constructions, which is entirely covered. In so far as we can find datable examples, most peasant huts throughout western and northern Britain continued to be of this kind, until at least Viking times. Small finds or extrinsic dating-methods alone distinguish them from their prehistoric counterparts. Yet one has a growing suspicion – reinforced by excavation in Ireland, particularly of domestic sites in Cos. Down and Antrim – that from pre-Roman Iron Age days, if from no earlier, a lesser and parallel tradition of rectilinear huts, involving quite advanced carpentry-work and mainly expressed in timber, existed; owing little or nothing to Roman models and forming an alternative architectural idiom in the post-Roman period. This may be notably so in (for instance) the case of dwellings and subsidiary buildings in the better-class settlements – the homes of substantial free farmers, or of lesser chieftains.

Much of our information is drawn from the archaeology of the early Church. While we cannot be absolutely sure of this, we assume that the individual living-cells of monastic brethren found in monasteries, communal hermitages, or developed cemeteries, are simply the ordinary secular house-types of the same era. This assumption highlights such obvious irregularities as the basically rectangular living-cells in the monastery at Tintagel, Cornwall. Are these, like so much else about Britain's earliest-dated monastery, really Mediterranean innovations?

Within the home, we can say comparatively little about furnishings. The hearth need not be central, but generally seems to be, as in prehistory. One partial indication of date is provided by the development of the stone hand-mill used for grinding the household flour – the rotary quern. By Late Roman times, rotary querns in Britain and Ireland generally had become much flatter than their Iron Age prototypes, a devolution of form which was to persist until the nineteenth century in the Outer Isles and one or two other remote spots. At some stage, the old method of propulsion – to sit cross-legged by the quern, and to turn it by grasping a short handle wedged near its circumference – gave way to a mechanically more efficient and less tiring, drive; a long staff, turning freely in two sockets (one directly above the quern, probably a hollow in a roof-beam, the other a hollow near the rim of the 96 upper stone), could be used to whirl the mill around. Further improvements include the use of several hollows on the quern in rotation to avoid uneven wear, and even the mounting of the quern on a kind of table, the pitch of milling being controlled by running a spindle from the upper stone down to a stone socket on a movable board. Hand-mills of this kind were in use in seventh-century Cornwall (and until Victorian times in the Isles of Scilly!) and upper quern stones, with the tell-tale hollows and rynd-slots for the spindle-head, come from post-Roman sites over most of Britain.

Farmers and Stockbreeders

The uneven historical emphasis that we tend to place on 'invasions', battles, sieges, and atypical events in general must not obscure the fact that the early British and Irish, like the Anglo-Saxon peoples and subsequently the Vikings, relied on the land for their sustenance. First and foremost they were farmers; some might, within their mixed economy, place greater reliance on pastoralism and stockbreeding, and a few specialized communities no doubt contained a high proportion of fishermen. It is thus extraordinary that we seem to know so little of our oldest industry at this time.

96 Reconstruction of a hand-mill, sixth–seventh centuries AD, from Gwithian, west Cornwall

In the Roman world (and this includes Roman Britain), agriculture had progressed far beyond the clumsy ard and the stone hoes of Bronze Age times, beyond the scratch-ploughs and the simple granaries of the Iron Age. The Roman farmers had not only a range of iron hand-tools almost as wide as that which we have now; they possessed farm carts, bush- and frame-harrows, moderately efficient ploughs (even wheeled ones), sledges, and a primitive reaping-machine (the *vallus*). Land-owning Roman gentlemen were expected to take an interest, either personally or through reliable bailiffs, in the working of their properties, and some elegant agrarian textbooks existed to guide them in this pursuit. A very wide selection of cereals, vegetables, and fruits were cultivated in Roman Britain, many for the first time.

Over three centuries or so, some of these improvements must have affected the British countryside, within and beyond the frontiers. Most signs of this contact are, unfortunately, to be dated late in the first millennium AD, if not indeed in the early Middle Ages; and while we know equally little about details of agricultural practice in the Anglo-Saxon world, we cannot be sure that objects and actions depicted in eleventh-century manuscripts necessarily reflect any continuity from post-Roman farming. Literary and legal-historical sources, both in Ireland and in the world of the early English, supplement our knowledge of a much more difficult topic; the relationship between, not fields as such, but types and patterns of field layout on the one hand, and varieties of land-tenure, settlement, and social groupings on the other.

There are rare exceptions, where fate has been kind to the archaeologist. A fairly heavy plough characterized by a coulter and a (fixed) mould-board, not necessarily wheeled but able to turn a furrow, was known in Roman Britain. Traces of one ancient field, its use dated by the fact that the manure spread over it contained broken

pottery among the household waste, were found at a
97 peasant homestead at Gwithian, west Cornwall; this field
was cultivated during the sixth and seventh centuries AD,
too early for any contact with Saxon Wessex, and because
it happened that the plough-soil lay directly over blown
sand, the contrast in colour revealed (in plan) actual
turned furrows. Here was a post-Roman Dumnonian
farmer, and a poor one, working marginal land, using a
mould-board – an improvement that can only have come
from, and survived from, Roman Britain.

Fields in highland Britain were not large. It must be
remembered that, in areas with much surface rock, both
the size of a field and the height and thickness of the stone
walls or banks which surround it are related to the amount
of surface stone which has, originally, to be cleared, and
to such factors as the need to provide wind-breaks and to
prevent stock from getting into arable ground. Nor
should we envisage anything like present-day crop yields;
detailed estimates, from both northern Ireland and Cornwall, suggest that a single family homestead in Roman
and post-Roman times, inhabiting some kind of enclosed
steading with appropriate buildings, may have required
upwards of forty acres of potential arable alone. Lastly,
as so often in fairly primitive communities, life was not
necessarily simple because it was crude. In both Welsh
and Cornish, there are extensive and presumably once-
specialized vocabularies for the agricultural life: Cornish
alone has nearly twenty words which could be translated
by the modern English 'field'.

Stockbreeding mainly involved cattle and sheep; in the
Anglo-Saxon world, domestic swine played an important
part, perhaps less so in the Celtic-speaking regions, where
wild boar survived until their semi-domestication during
the Middle Ages. The dog, first employed as the stockbreeder's partner in Neolithic times, had long since
separated into a whole variety of breeds, the humbler

Preserved by an accident of fate (contrasting layers of sand and plough-soil), these turned plough-furrows from Gwithian, west Cornwall, were made some time during the sixth–eighth centuries A D

sorts still working-dogs on the farms and pastures, larger and specialized beasts becoming hunting-dogs, wolf-hounds, and aristocratic accessories. Domestic herds, which comprised breeds of both sheep and cattle considerably smaller than anything we expect to see today, still had their natural enemies; setting aside such curiosities as the European lynx and the brown bear, both of which may have lingered on until Roman times or afterwards, the wolf was the major menace. The late R. A. S. Macalister quoted a very strange anecdote, which would place the extinction of the wolf in Ireland closer to 1800 than to the usual date (1710)!

Cattle, in particular, possessed a significance over and above their straightforward value for milk, flesh, and leather. In early Ireland, as in the outer *civitates* of Roman Britain (like Brigantia, or Dumnonia), cattle were also wealth, a concept reminding us that Latin *pecunia*, 'money, property', is directly linked to the Latin *pecus*, 'cattle, domesticated beast'. This leads to further connections with status (within a stratified society), units of value based on livestock, and a commercial system not based on coinage. We could, though we need not, take this much further back to a Celtic Iron Age where the bull could be a divine symbol and where herds of cattle possibly constituted the only certain display of large-scale wealth.

Horses – and here one must picture little shaggy creatures, like Exmoors or large Shetlands – played several parts in post-Roman life. Oxen, gelded male cattle, were employed for heavy draught; Cogitosus' *Life of St Brigit*, a seventh-century work, describes an ox-team belonging to Kildare monastery, sent out to the nearby Red Hills to drag home a full-sized millstone, and other ox-teams would certainly have become increasingly used for ploughing. Horses, if we can call these Celtic ponies such, had a separate story in this respect, having been set aside in the early Celtic world to draw light war-chariots, harnessed side by side. While this practice died out in Gaul in the last centuries BC, and in most of Britain during the first century AD, it was kept up in Ireland until rather later. A recent analysis by Professor David Greene suggests that the 'chariot' of Early Christian Ireland, a vehicle which figures prominently in the heroic literature, had come to resemble something more like a modern donkey-shay – a shallow box on two smallish wheels. Now this may have been widely current, in differing forms, over much of post-Roman Britain; horse-drawn, and used both as a light farm-cart and as a means of travel.

98   The Papil shrine-panel, Shetland (early eighth century); monks process towards a cross. The horseman may be a bishop

Certain Pictish Class II stones, if not copying from imported ivories or manuscripts, show this; such vehicles also figure in a number of Saints' Lives, in connection with Scotland, Ireland, and Cornwall. They do not necessarily imply metalled roads, but the references to them do suggest that these carts or carriages were nothing out of the ordinary.

The horse was, of course, also the riding-animal of the well-to-do. Pictish persons of quality are frequently shown, on Class II symbol stones, mounted on ponies, having broad saddle-cloths and perhaps box-stirrups attached to the front corners of these cloths. This attribute was carried over into the Christian world; a mounted cleric, probably a bishop, appears on an eighth-century shrine panel from Shetland, and in the seventh century, *98* Bishop Aidan of Northumbria was given a very fine horse by King Oswin, on which he could ride around his diocese. When the saintly Aidan gave this horse away to the first beggar he met, Oswin chided him, and asked whether one of the many less valuable horses of other kinds in the royal herds would not have fulfilled this charity as well. We see here at least a hint of selective breeding by this date. Lastly, the horse could have been a solitary domestic beast of burden. In Adomnán's *Life of St Columba* (about 680) there is a touching story of Columba's last days on Iona, when he was accosted by a white horse, 'the obedient servant who was accustomed to carry the milk-vessels between the pasture and the monastery'.

One can say little about goats, probably still feral in both Britain and Ireland, because of the difficulties of sorting out their bones from those of sheep; but there must be a mention of the cat. The domestic (Mediterranean) cat was introduced by the Romans. One suspects that, by Viking times, it was far from rare in Britain, and the value attached to it was due to its prowess in dealing with rats and mice around the home and the granary.

Men of Special Gifts

In early Irish society, certain persons stood on one side of a long stratification from the various grades of king down to the unfree serf. These included bards, seers, judges, historians – successors to what are popularly grouped together as 'druids' in an earlier Celtic world – and there are grounds for including with them the master-craftsmen, the skilled wrights and jewellers. *Aes dána*, 'men of special gifts', is the appropriate term.

The minor artefacts of the post-Roman world, from Ireland, from Celtic Britain, from Anglo-Saxon England, are not only distinctly uninspiring; they are often distinctly uninformative, and (to take a simple instance) small one-edged iron knives all look very similar at this time, whichever cultural area they may belong to. Only in the largely unexplored world of weapons, horse-furniture (poorly represented in the archaeological record), and above all, jewellery, do we detect regional differences corresponding to earlier cultural traditions, and the hands of individual craftsmen.

The finest pieces of workmanship, employing not only gold and silver, but the contrast afforded by glass, enamel, niello, crystal, semi-precious stones, and the variations of light and shade produced by working or engraving the metal surfaces, are concerned with personal adornment. This statement excludes, of course, a smaller *102, 103* class of specifically Christian purpose, such as chalices.

Analogies from the Middle Ages suggest that certain very notable craftsmen produced exceptional pieces for kings, princes, and their womenfolk, and were for this purpose attached to a household. The evidence for *ateliers*, or permanent craft workshops with controlled apprenticeships, is perhaps stronger in Anglo-Saxon contexts – especially the Jutish and Frankish sphere of Kent – than it is in Celtic Britain or in Ireland.

Without being side-tracked into the discussion of the prehistory of trousers – a fascinating byway of the past – one must relate jewellery to dress. Post-Roman Britain and Ireland, and this is a safe generality, was sartorially dominated by the wrap-around garment (as opposed to the shaped, buttoned, garment). The outer woollen cloak (the Irish *brat*) had been a product of Roman Britain whose fame as a barrier to wind and rain had attracted notice in other parts of the Empire. This, and any inner garment which, like the Mediterranean toga or *chlamys*, was merely secured by pinning or tucking-in its last fold, could be fastened with a long pin pushed through the fabric. The safety-pin, as we now know it, was in use for some such purpose over much of Europe in the pre-Roman Iron Age, and the history of costume jewellery is really the history of the garment-securing pin, with its lesser cousin the brooch (a pin whose point is not free, but moves back to engage in a catch-plate).

Early Anglo-Saxon jewellery, mostly of the brooch class, exemplifies the blend of traditions behind these crafts. From the Mediterranean world of Greece and Rome, diffused through early colonies, through barbarian contact, and through military service, a technique known as 'chip-carving' – treatment of a metal surface in a way reminiscent of wood-working – and a variety of modified animal ornaments eventually found their way into the Anglo-Saxon repertoire. Abstract forms and designs, culminating in numerous styles of knots and

104, 105

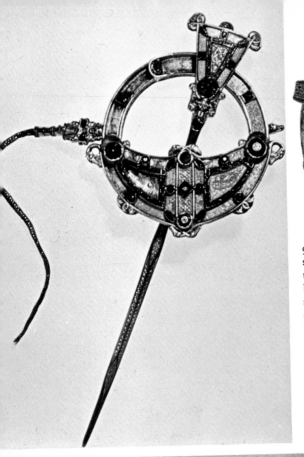

99–101 *Left*, the Tara Brooch, a superb example of Irish art. *Above*, the Breadalbane Brooch, an Irish brooch converted (in Scotland?) into a Pictish type by altering the pin and cutting away the strap between the terminals. *Below*, two of the silver brooches from the St Ninian's Isle hoard; specifically Pictish forms, with characteristic terminals

102 *Right*, the eighth-century Ardagh Chalice, greatest of the ecclesiastical altar vessels

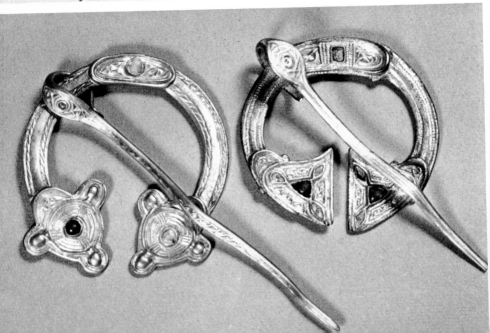

interlace, and an attractive habit of heightening the visual effect with inset pieces of brightly coloured stone, glass, or other media, betray ancestral northern European styles and the influence of Celtic British tastes which had themselves already affected Roman provincial metalwork. *108, 109* In Kent and eastern parts of England, superb 'poly- *106, 107* chrome' jewellery, as the pieces inlaid with colour are called, mostly dates from the late sixth to the early eighth century.

The native British forms show the development of the straight pin, which becomes long and elaborate, with intricate treatment of enlarged and complex heads; and of the so-called 'penannular brooch', where (from a start in *99–101* prehistory) a loose ring through the pin's head grows to become an enlarged partial ring around whose centre a subsidiary pin can swivel. As well as bronze (and iron,

103–105   *Left*, a plain silver chalice: the Trewhiddle (Cornwall) Chalice, 5 inches high, from a hoard deposited *c.* 875. *Opposite*, parallel elaboration in manuscript and metalwork: initial from the Lindisfarne Gospels, and part of the Sutton Hoo gold buckle. The interlaced dragon-like creatures, common to both schemes, also occur on stone in Pictish art

which normally does not survive intact), silver and even gold were used, the highlights being certain very fine Scottish silver pieces and such unique creations as the Irish 'Tara' brooch.

Much more mysterious are objects like hanging-bowls, which (and this is to some extent true of jewellery styles) are found in both British and Anglo-Saxon contexts – the latter often graves. Hanging-bowls are shallow metal bowls, usually with three equally spaced rings around the rim, that were suspended from tripods – not unlike modern camping wash-basins. Argument as to their purpose – votive chalices, lamps, hand-basins, serving-bowls, drinking-vessels, even ornaments – is unending, and obviously a multiple use is probable. On balance, it seems most likely that these originated in Roman models, and were produced until the seventh century, if not later, mainly by British craftsmen for both British (including Irish) and Anglo-Saxon users. What complicates the issue *108* is that the 'escutcheons', the strengthening-plates at the ring-sockets, display a very wide range of art motifs, some of which – as in the Pictish Class I and II symbol stones – show how the vocabulary of pre-Roman Celtic art was partly maintained for the best part of a thousand years. Escutcheons, torn off and found alone, may at one stage have ornamented pagan Saxon warriors.

In the far north, there is a small and remarkable group of objects, apparently made from surviving silver and silver-gilt Roman vessels and other items. These are distinguished by their massiveness, and by the appearance of the familiar Pictish symbols engraved on them and sometimes heightened with red enamel. The great Pictish chains are surely marks of kingship or chieftaincy, but other pieces, like the odd little 'lappets', have not yet been explained.

Warriors and Mercenaries

At various times in the British and Irish past, various personal weapons have enjoyed prolonged popularity. There are fashions in this, as in most human activities. It would be fair to say that the post-Roman period was dominated by forms of sword and spear, rather than by daggers or slings or bows. The typology of this subject has yet to be worked out.

The bow – the full-length long-bow, which has to be strung and bent – goes back to the Early Bronze Age at least. Recovery of prehistoric or early bows is a matter of luck, and rarely happens. Whether the long-bow did or did not survive in Wales to become Britain's salvation at Crécy and Agincourt is a matter of pure conjecture; if it did, it did so as a hunting and sporting weapon. Pictish Class II stones have figure-scenes with bowmen, but engaged in the chase (of deer), and their bows are the curved, small, probably composite type, originating in Asia for use on horseback and passed to the Early Iron Age world of the Celts through contact with Eurasiatic peoples in central Europe.

The spear, a long-shafted weapon with an elongated iron head, a weapon which was widely current at the end

106, 107 The Kingston Brooch, *left*; seventh-century, 84 mm across, set with garnets and lapis lazuli. *Right*, the ninth-century Alfred Jewel portrays the great king; it reads AELFRED MEC HEHT GEWYRCAN ('Alfred had me wrought')

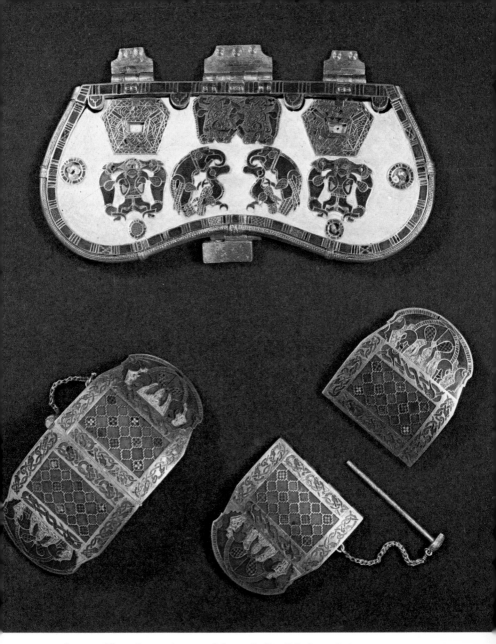

108, 109   The aristocratic arts of the early English drew their ornament from many sources. *Left*, the hanging-bowl escutcheon, from the Sutton Hoo ship-burial; despite years of argument, the provenance of hanging-bowls remains unsettled, but surviving Celtic motifs predominate in the ornamented escutcheons. The Sutton Hoo grave-goods include, *above*, the graceful purse-lid, the gold offset by garnets and coloured glass; the motifs, perhaps cult-scenes, include 'Daniel in the Lion's Den'. Of special magnificence, appropriate to a king, are the two heavy gold clasps, each secured by a link-pin on a chain of the Bronze Age, must have survived in native hands throughout the Iron Age and Roman periods – spears are cheaper to mass-produce than swords – and, notably in Ireland and North Britain, appears to have been the foot-soldier's basic armament in Post-Roman times. Iron spearheads are not uncommon from sites like Dunadd, or the major Irish excavations of this period, and spears frequently figure on Pictish Class II figure-scenes.

Anglo-Saxon spearheads, which have again never been fully studied, are quite common: the early English did in fact use the long-bow, possibly for warfare as well as the chase, but we do not know how widely. An essentially Germanic, non-British, weapon was the iron battle-axe: this could be the *francisca*, a small curved throwing-axe of the tomahawk class, or a larger object like that traditionally used by medieval executioners, and even axes with exaggeratedly long blades in T-form. These must to some extent have also been the carpenters' and foresters' tools.

Swords exhibit tremendous variety. In the entire range of length, we begin with the dagger and dirk class, larger than any form of eating-knife, which in British hands were not unlike later medieval daggers, as far as we can tell. Germanic peoples had rather more specialized forms, some of which were given greater weight by being one-edged, with a heavy flat back to the blade which was generally about 15 to 20 ins long; this is the Anglo-Saxon *scramasax*. The full-length sword was universally employed. Some early ones recall the clumsy *spatha* of the Roman auxiliaries; but there are superb objects with names and words inlaid or inscribed on the blade, and elaborate hilts.

A final and rather puzzling aspect of warriorhood is the possibility that mercenary soldiers were more common than we suppose, and that the archaeological record can be confused if weapons proper to people of area *A* turn

110 No doubt surrounds this long iron sword from Ballinderry, Co. Westmeath, a ninth-century Viking type whose patterned guard bears the name HILTEPREHT

up, in acceptably normal contexts, within area *B*. Literary sources, particularly Irish ones, are not terribly helpful here, because of imprecision as to external affairs; 'Gauls' and 'Franks' do not necessarily carry exact connotations, and a phrase like the Irish *i tírib gallaib* ('in the lands of the Gauls'), may, at this stage, really mean no more than 'abroad' or 'foreign parts'.

This is important because several large Irish sites have produced exotic objects. Lagore, a royal site in Leinster, yielded many finds of arms and weapons, some clearly Irish, others in the past labelled as Viking because they appear to be Germanic. Careful reassessment of the dating evidence suggests that some, at least, of this material may really be seventh or early eighth century. If so, given our increased knowledge of the kind of swords and spears then current in (say) Frankish and Merovingian lands, these are more likely to represent imported arms, or better, the arms of European mercenaries. Not too much weight can be laid on this, though there are other post-Roman British sites – Dinas Powys, in Glamorgan – where Anglo-Saxon or Germanic objects might be explained along these lines. In his classic study of the earliest Welsh poetry, Sir Ifor Williams drew attention to linguistic evidence for 'Frankish' mercenaries in Ireland – there are such words as *amus* or *amhus*, 'mercenary', *francamus*, '(?) Frankish mercenary' – and to the context of a Welsh fragment of the early ninth century. In this, a defeated chief speaks from his deserted hall; he is alone, save for 'his Frank', whom he despises; 'Mean is my company'. 'I cannot see', Sir Ifor wrote, 'any flagrant impossibility in the supposition that exiled or wandering Frankish warriors may have occasionally crossed the seas and enlisted in the service of Welsh and Irish chiefs.' In view of the intensified contact now suggested by archaeological study, was this perhaps an aspect of service that we have, so far, underestimated?

Select Bibliography

This select list of books, arranged loosely under the main subject-headings, is intended mainly as a guide to further reading, and is deliberately weighted in the direction of those books which themselves contain extensive bibliographies. References to articles in periodicals and journals have been included only when no other source exists; for the general reader, certain works written in Welsh or in the less familiar European languages have been omitted.

Structure of Roman Britain

RICHMOND, I. A., *Roman Britain*, Pelican History of England, Harmondsworth 1955.
RIVET, A. L. F., *Town and Country in Roman Britain*, London 1958
RICHMOND, I. A., ed., *Roman and Native in North Britain*, London 1958.
SALWAY, P., *The Frontier People of Roman Britain*, Cambridge 1965.
WACHER, J. S., ed., *Civitas Capitals of Roman Britain*, Leicester 1966.
THOMAS, C., ed., *Rural Settlement in Roman Britain*, CBA Research Report no. 7, London 1966.
FRERE, S. S., *Britannia*, History of the Roman Provinces, London 1967.
COLLINGWOOD, R. G. and RICHMOND, I. A., *The Archaeology of Roman Britain*, 2nd rev. edn., London 1969.
ORDNANCE SURVEY, *Map of Roman Britain*, 3rd edn., London 1956.

Roman Religion and Art

TOYNBEE, J. M. C., *Art in Roman Britain*, London 1962.
—, *Art in Britain under the Romans*, Oxford 1964.
HARRIS, J. R. and E., *Oriental Cults in Roman Britain*, Leiden 1965.
LEWIS, M. J. T., *Temples in Roman Britain*, Cambridge 1966.
TOYNBEE, J. M. C., *Death and Burial in the Roman World*, London 1971

Native Principalities

CHADWICK, N. K., ed., *Studies in Early British History*, Cambridge 1959.
CHADWICK, N. K., *Celtic Britain*, London 1963.
MORRIS, J., 'Dark Age Dates' in *Britain and Rome – Studies presented to Eric Birley*, ed. M. G. JARRETT and B. DOBSON, Kendal 1966, 145–85.
BINCHY, D. A., *Celtic and Anglo-Saxon Kingship*, O'Donnell Lectures 1967–8, Oxford 1970.

Linguistics

JACKSON, K. H., *Language and History in Early Britain*, Edinburgh 1953.
—, 'The Pictish Language', in *The Problem of the Picts*, ed. F. T. WAINWRIGHT, Edinburgh and London 1955.
GREENE, D., 'The Celtic Languages', in *The Celts*, Thomas Davis Lectures 1960, ed. J. RAFTERY, Cork 1964, 9–22.
—, 'The Making of Insular Celtic', in *Proceedings 2nd International Congress of Celtic Studies*, Cardiff 1966, 123–36.

The Anglo-Saxons

STENTON, F. M., *Anglo-Saxon England*, 2nd edn., Oxford 1947.
HUNTER BLAIR, P., *An Introduction to Anglo-Saxon England*, Cambridge 1956.

WILSON, D. M., *The Anglo-Saxons*, London 1960.
LOYN, H. R., *Anglo-Saxon England and The Norman Conquest*, London 1962.
HUNTER BLAIR, P., *Roman Britain and Early England*, Edinburgh 1963.
MYRES, J. N. L., *Anglo-Saxon Pottery and the Settlement of England*, Oxford 1969.

Special Aspects

HAWKES, S. C. and DUNNING, G. C., 'Soldiers and settlers in Britain, fourth to fifth century', in *Medieval Archaeology*, V (1961), 1–70.
GELLING, M., 'English place-names derived from the compound *wīchám*, in *Medieval Archaeology*, XI (1967), 87–104.

'King Arthur'

LOOMIS, R. S., *Wales and the Arthurian Legend*, Cardiff 1956.
LOOMIS, R. S., ed., *Arthurian Literature in the Middle Ages*, Oxford 1959.
JONES, T., 'The early evolution of the legend of Arthur', in *Nottingham Medieval Studies*, VIII (1964), 3–21.
ASHE, G., ed., *The Quest for Arthur's Britain*, London 1968.
HIBBERT, C., *The Search For King Arthur*, New York 1969.

The Picts

WAINWRIGHT, F. T., ed., *The Problem of the Picts*, Edinburgh and London 1955.
THOMAS, C., 'The interpretation of the Pictish symbols', in *Archaeological Journal*, CXX (1963), 31–97.
CRUDEN, S. E., *The Early Christian and Pictish Monuments of Scotland*, Edinburgh 1964.
HENDERSON, I., *The Picts*, London 1967.

The Scots

ANDERSON, A. O., *Early Sources of Scottish History*, 2 vols., Edinburgh 1922.
CHADWICK, N. K., *Celtic Britain*, London 1963, chap. iii.

Wales and Mann

WILLIAMS, A. H., *An Introduction to the History of Wales*, vol. I, Cardiff 1962.
REES, W., *An Historical Atlas of Wales*, rev. edn., London 1959.
FOSTER, I. LL. and DANIEL, G. E., eds., *Prehistoric and Early Wales*, London 1965, chaps. vi–vii.
KINVIG, R. H., *A History of the Isle of Man*, 2nd ed., Liverpool 1950.
RICHARD, M., 'The Irish settlements in south-west Wales, a topographical approach', in *Journal of the Royal Society of Antiquaries of Ireland*, XC (1960), 133–52.

South-West Britain

TAYLOR, T., *The Celtic Christianity of Cornwall*, London 1916.
THOMAS, C., *Christian Antiquities of Camborne*, St Austell 1967, chaps. iii–vi.
—, 'Grass-marked pottery', in *Studies in Ancient Europe – essays presented to Stuart Piggott*, ed. J. M. COLES and D. D. A. SIMPSON, Leicester 1968, 311–32.

Brittany and Galicia

HEMON, R., *La langue bretonne et ses combats*, La Baule 1947.
JACKSON, K. H., *Language and History in Early Britain*, Edinburgh 1953, chap. i.
CHADWICK, N. K., 'The colonization of Brittany from Celtic Britain', in *Proceedings of the British Academy*, LI (1967), 235–99.
—, *Early Brittany*, Cardiff 1969.

Christianity in Celtic Britain

WILLIAMS, H., *Christianity in Early Britain*, Oxford 1912.
GOUGAUD, L., *Christianity in Celtic Lands*, London 1932.
CHADWICK, N.K., ed., *Studies in the Early British Church*, Cambridge 1958.
CHADWICK, N.K., *The Age of the Saints in the Early Celtic Church*, Riddell Lectures 1960, London 1961.
BARLEY, M.W., and HANSON, R.P.C., ed., *Christianity in Britain 300–700*, Leicester 1968.

Christianity in the English Settlements

MASON, A.J., ed., *The Mission of St Augustine to England*, Cambridge 1897.
THOMPSON, A.H., ed., *Bede – his life, times and writings*, Oxford 1935.
LEVISON, W., *England and the Continent in the Eighth Century*, Ford Lectures 1943, Oxford 1946.
DEANESLY, M., *The Pre-Conquest Church in England*, London 1961.
GODFREY, C., *The Church in Anglo-Saxon England*, Cambridge 1962.

Christian archaeology and architecture

LEASK, H.G., *Irish Churches and Monastic Buildings*, vol. 1, Dundalk 1955.
TAYLOR, H.M. and J., *Anglo-Saxon Architecture*, 2 vols., Cambridge 1965.
THOMAS, C., *The Early Christian Archaeology of North Britain*, Hunter Marshall Lectures 1968, Oxford 1971.

Early Christian Ireland

RYAN, J., *Irish Monasticism*, Dublin 1931.
DE PAOR, M. and L., *Early Christian Ireland*, London 1958.
BIELER, L., *Ireland – Harbinger of the Middle Ages*, London 1963.
HUGHES, K., *The Church in Early Irish Society*, London 1966.
NORMAN, E.R., and ST. JOSEPH, J.K.S., *The Early Development of Irish Society – the evidence of aerial photography*, Cambridge 1969.
ORDNANCE SURVEY (DUBLIN), *Map of Monastic Ireland*, 2nd edn., Dublin 1964.

St Ninian

MACQUEEN, J., *St Nynia*, Edinburgh and London 1961.

St Patrick

BURY, J.B., *The Life of St Patrick and his place in history*, London 1905.
MACNEILL, E., *St Patrick*, ed. J. RYAN, Dublin 1964.
BIELER, L., *The Life and Legend of St Patrick*, Dublin 1949.
RYAN, J., ed., *St Patrick*, Thomas Davis Lectures, Dublin 1958.
BINCHY, D.A., 'St Patrick and his biographers; ancient and modern', in *Studia Hibernica*, II (1962), 7–173.
BIELER, L., *St Patrick and the coming of Christianity*, History of Irish Catholicism, vol. 1, Dublin 1967.
HANSON, R.P.C., *St Patrick: his origins and career*, Oxford 1968.

Literary Sources – Celtic

DILLON, M., ed., *Irish Sagas*, Thomas Davis Lectures, Dublin 1959.
O'RAHILLY, C., *Táin Bó Cúalnge, from the Book of Leinster*, Dublin 1967.
WILLIAMS, I., ed. WILLIAMS, J.E.C., *The Poems of Taliesin*, Dublin 1968.
JACKSON, K.H., *The Gododdin – the oldest Scottish poem*, Edinburgh 1969.
KENNEY, J.F., *The sources for the early history of Ireland*; vol. 1, *Ecclesiastical*, New York 1929, repr.

REEVES, W., *The Life of St Columba, written by Adamnan*, Dublin 1857.
ANDERSON, A.O. and M.O., *Adomnán's life of Columba*, London 1961.
WADE-EVANS, A.W., *Vitae sanctorum Britanniae et genealogiae*, Cardiff 1944.
BIELER, L., *The Early Irish Penitentials (Scriptores Latini Hiberniae, V)*, Dublin 1963.

Literary Sources – English

HADDAN, A.W. and STUBBS, W., *Councils and ecclesiastical documents relating to Great Britain and Ireland*, 3 vols., Oxford 1869 (repr. 1964).
WHITELOCK, D., ed., *English Historical Documents*, c. 500–1042, vol. I, London 1955.
—, *The Anglo-Saxon Chronicle*, London 1961.
WRIGHT, D., *Beowulf – a prose translation*, Harmondsworth 1957.
GORDON, R.K., *Anglo-Saxon poetry*, rev. edn., London 1954.
KENNEDY, C.W., *Early English Christian poetry*, New York 1963.
SHERLEY-PRICE, L., *Bede – A History of the English Church and People*, Harmondsworth 1955.
COLGRAVE, B., and MYNORS, R.A.B., *Bede's Ecclesiastical History of the English People*, Oxford 1969.
COLGRAVE, B., *The life of Bishop Wilfrid by Eddius Stephanus*, Cambridge 1927.
—, *Two Lives of St Cuthbert*, Cambridge 1940.
WEBB, J.F., *Lives of the Saints – Voyage of St Brendan, Bede's Life of Cuthbert, Eddius Stephanus' Life of Wilfrid*, Harmondsworth 1965.

Art

ROMILLY ALLEN, J., *Celtic art in pagan and Christian times*, London 1904.
HENRY, F., *Irish art in the Early Christian period*, London 1940.
—, *Irish art in the Early Christian period to A.D. 800*, London 1965.
LEEDS, E.T., *Celtic ornament in the British Isles down to A.D. 700*, Oxford 1933.
KENDRICK, T.D., *Anglo-Saxon Art to 900*, London 1938.

Special topics

NASH-WILLIAMS, V.E., *The Early Christian Monuments of Wales*, Cardiff 1950.
BATTISCOMBE, C.F., ed., *The relics of St Cuthbert – studies by various authors*, Oxford 1956.
BRUCE-MITFORD, R.L.S., *The Sutton Hoo ship burial, a handbook*, new edn., London 1968.
GREEN, C., *Sutton Hoo, the excavation of a royal ship burial*, London 1963.
O'DELL, A.C., *et al.*, *The St. Ninian's Isle Treasure*, Edinburgh 1960.

Archaeology of sites and homesteads

HARDEN, D.B., ed., *Dark-Age Britain – studies presented to E.T. Leeds*, London 1956.
DE PAOR, M. and L., *Early Christian Ireland*, London 1958.
WILSON, D.M., *The Anglo-Saxons*, London 1960.
EVANS, E.E., *Prehistoric and Early Christian Ireland, a guide*, London 1966.
ALCOCK, L., *Dinas Powys*, Cardiff 1963.

Periodicals

Excavation reports on individual sites may appear anywhere, most frequently in county journals, but *Medieval Archaeology* (London: Society for Medieval Archaeology) covers the post-Roman period and contains annual chronicles of work in progress and of results. The major Irish periodicals for this period are *Proceedings of the Royal Irish Academy, section C* (Dublin), *Journal of the Royal Society of Antiquaries of Ireland* (Dublin), and *Ulster Journal of Archaeology* (Belfast). Scotland and Wales are covered by *Proceedings of the Society of Antiquaries of Scotland* (Edinburgh), and *Archaeologia Cambrensis* (Cardiff). *Bulletin of the Board of Celtic Studies* (Cardiff), partly in Welsh, also covers both early history and archaeology. From 1971, a new annual, *Britannia* (London), will contain major articles on Roman (including, possibly, sub-Roman) Britain.

List of Illustrations

The author and publishers are grateful to the many official bodies, institutions and individuals mentioned below for their assistance in supplying illustration material. Illustrations without acknowledgment are from original material in the archives of Thames and Hudson. BM= British Museum; DE=Department of the Environment, crown copyright reserved; AM= Ashmolean Museum, Oxford; St J=Dr J.K. St Joseph, crown copyright reserved; NMA= National Museum of Antiquities of Scotland; NMI= National Museum of Ireland.

1 Map of sixth- and seventh-century migrations. Drawn by John Woodcock

2 Gold *solidus* of Constantine III. *BM.* Photo Peter Clayton

3 Gold *solidus* of Magnus Maximus. *BM.* Photo Peter Clayton

4 Ivory diptych panel. Cathedral Treasury, Monza. Photo Mansell-Alinari Collection

5 Hadrian's Wall. Photo *DE*

6 Map of the Saxon Shore forts. Drawn by Cecilia Fellner

7 Portchester Castle. Photo *DE*

8 Burgh Castle. Photo *DE*

9 Fifth-century Verulamium. Drawn by Susan Mercer after Frere

10 Fifth-century coins from Lydney. Photo courtesy of the Society of Antiquaries, London

11 Romano-British buckle from Gwithian. Photo F.M.B. Cooke

12 Political map of Roman Britain. Drawn by S. Schotten after Rivet

13 Cubert tombstone. Drawn by the author after Macalister

14 Silver coin of Caratacus. *BM.* Photo Ray Gardner

15 Tombstone of Rufus Sita, Gloucester. Photo the Warburg Institute

16 Finds from a grave at Dorchester. *AM.* Museum photo

17 Distribution-map of Germanic settlements. Drawn by S. Schotten after Myres

18 Germanic and Anglo-Saxon pottery. Drawn by Cecilia Fellner after Myres

19 Offa's Dyke, Llanfair Waterdine, Salop. Photo *St J*

20 Distribution-map of Celtic river names. Drawn by S. Schotten after Jackson

21 Birdoswald fort. Photo *St J*

22 Badbury Rings. Photo *St J*

23 The Mounth. Photo John Leng & Co. Ltd

24 Distribution-map of place-name elements 'Pit'. Drawn by S. Schotten after Jackson

25 Distribution-map of brochs, crannogs and souterrains. Drawn by S. Schotten after Stevenson

26 Souterrain at Carn Euny, Cornwall. Photo Charles Woolf

27 Souterrain at Ardestie, Angus. Photo *DE*

28 Distribution-map of Pictish Class I stones. After Henderson

29 Symbols on Pictish Class I stones. The author

30 Pictish stone from Glamis Manse. Photo
 DE

31 Pictish stone from Dunnichen, Angus.
 NMA, Edinburgh. Museum photo

32 Pictish stone from Easterton of
 Roseisle. *NMA*, Edinburgh. Museum
 photo

33 Interior of broch, Jarlshof. Photo *DE*

34 Broch of Mousa. Photo *DE*

35 Silver strap-terminals, St Ninian's Isle.
 NMA, Edinburgh. Photo courtesy of
 the Trustees of the British Museum

36 Detail from Adamnan's Life of Columba.
 Photo courtesy Stiftsbibliothek, St
 Gallen, Switzerland

37 Bronze head, Iona. Photo F. M. B. Cooke

38 Rock of Dunadd

39 Dunnottar Rock, Kincardineshire

40 Souterrain ware. Drawn by Miss G. D.
 Jones after the author

41 Grass-marked pottery. Drawn by Miss
 G. D. Jones after the author

42 Distribution-map of Irish place-name
 elements. Drawn by S. Schotten after
 Nicolaisen and Richards

43 Calf of Man Crucifixion. Photo Manx
 Museum

44 Crux Guriat. Photo Manx Museum

45 Gravestone of Voteporix

46 Gravestone of Quenataucus

47, 48 Tombstone from Ivybridge, Devon.
 BM. Photos courtesy of the Trustees of
 the British Museum

49 The Men Scryfys

50 The Doniert Stone. Photo Peter Chèze-
 Brown

51 Distribution-map of Christian fixtures.

Drawn by S. Schotten after the author

52 Icklingham lead tank. *BM*. Photo Peter
 Clayton

53 Wall-painting of chi-rho monogram,
 Lullingstone Villa. *BM*. Photo Peter
 Clayton

54 Wall-painting of an *orans*. Lullingstone
 Villa. *BM*. Photo Peter Clayton

55 Hinton St Mary mosaic. *BM*. Photo Royal
 Commission on Historical Monuments

56 Tombstone from St Just-in-Penwith.
 Photo Peter Chèze-Brown

57 Initial from Bede's Life of St Cuthbert.
 Bodleian Library, Oxford

58, 59 Physgill Cave. Photos *DE*

60 Distribution-map of imported Mediterranean pottery. Drawn by S. Schotten
 after the author

61 Distribution-map of imported amphorae.
 Drawn by S. Schotten after the author

62 Tintagel. Photo Aerofilms Ltd

63 Initial from the Cathach of St Columba.
 Photo Royal Irish Academy, Dublin

64 Muiredach's Cross, Monasterboice. Photo
 Edwin Smith

65 Lough Erne figure. Photo *Impartial
 Reporter*, Inniskillen

66 Monymusk Reliquary. *NMA*, Edinburgh. Museum photo

67 Athlone Crucifixion, *NMI*, Dublin.
 Museum photo

68 Rupertus Cross. Photo Bayerisches
 Nationalmuseum, Munich

69 Sceilg Mhichíl. Bord Failte Photo, Irish
 Tourist Board

70 Sceilg Mhichíl monastery. Photo *St J*

71 Gold *solidus* of Wigmund. *BM*. Photo
 Peter Clayton

72 Pectoral cross of St Cuthbert. Durham Cathedral Library. Photo Colourslide Centre, Slough

73 Portrait of St Dunstan. Bodleian Library, Oxford

74 Carpet page from Lindisfarne Gospels. *BM*. Photo Eileen Tweedy

75 Benedictional of St Aethelwold. *BM*. Photo courtesy of the Trustees of the British Museum

76 Brixworth Church. Photo Edwin Smith

77 Hexham Abbey. After H. and J. Taylor

78 Frith Stool, Hexham Abbey. Photo Walter Scott, Bradford

79 Echternach Gospels. Bibliothèque Nationale, Paris

80 Book of Durrow. Urs Graf Verlag

81 Book of Kells. Trinity College Library, Dublin

82 Tombstone from Hayle. The author after Macalister

83 Tombstone from Whithorn. The author after Macalister

84 Saturninus inscription

85 Ogam alphabet. Drawn by Miss G. D. Jones after the author

86 Ogam tombstone. After Macalister

87 Church Island, Co. Kerry. After O'Kelly

88 Moyne Graveyard. Photo *St J*

89 Kirkmaiden Cemetery. The author

90 Glamis Manse stone. Photo *DE*

91 Ruthwell Cross, detail. Photo Edwin Smith

92 Tap o' Noth. Photo *St J*

93 Dumbarton Rock. Photo *DE*

94 Traprain Law. Photo Malcolm Murray, Department of Archaeology, Edinburgh

95 Castle Dore. Photo *St J*

96 Gwithian hand-mill. Drawn by Miss G. D. Jones after the author

97 Plough-furrows, Gwithian. Photo J.V.S. Megaw

98 Papil shrine-panel. After Wainwright

99 Tara Brooch. *NMI*, Dublin. Museum photo

100 Breadalbane Brooch. *BM*. Photo courtesy of the Trustees of the British Museum

101 St Ninian's Isle brooches. *NMA*, Edinburgh. Photo Colourslide Centre, Slough

102 Ardagh Chalice, *NMI*, Dublin. Museum photo

103 Trewhiddle Chalice. *BM*. Photo courtesy of the Trustees of the British Museum

104 Lindisfarne Gospels, Initial. *BM*. Photo courtesy of the Trustees of the British Museum

105 Sutton Hoo gold buckle, detail. *BM*. Photo courtesy of the Trustees of the British Museum

106 Kingston Brooch. City of Liverpool Museums. Museum photo

107 Alfred Jewel. *AM*. Museum photo

108 Sutton Hoo hanging-bowl, detail. *BM*. Photo Peter Clayton

109 Sutton Hoo purse-lid and clasps. *BM*. Photo Eileen Tweedy

110 Viking sword from Ballinderry. *NMI*, Dublin. Museum photo

Index

Numbers in *italics* refer to illustrations.

aron, martyr, 72
bercorn, 82, 92
damnan (Adomnán), 53
delphius, bishop, 78
s dána, 126
gricultural implements, 121
idan, bishop, 91, 99, 102,
  125
lban, St, 72
lemanni, 31
mbrosius Aurelianus, 117
Innales Cambriae, 39–40
rles, Council of, 78, 80
rminius, deacon, 78
rmorica, 67
rthur, 38–42, 117
ugustine, St, 82, 95–8

amburgh, 99
anna (venta), 83
ede, Venerable, 21, 33, 53,
  78–9, 96–9, 102; *57*
ernicia, 27
lood-groups, 52–3
under, 66
ows, 131
recon (Brecknock), 59, 64
enin, brentyn, 26
reton language, 67–8
rigantinos, 26
ritish language, 28
ritonensis ecclesia, 70
rittany, 67

aergwbi, 90
aerleon, 72
alpornius, 25
amlann, 40–1
andida Casa, 79
anterbury, 9, 95–6
aratacus 26–7; *14*
arlisle, 19, 80, 82
astle Dore, 116; *95*
ts, 126
ttle, 124–5

cellae, 111
cemeteries, 109–11; *87–9*
chariots, 124
Chi-Rho symbol, 74; *52, 53,
  55, 56*
Ciarán, 90
cill, 58
Cirencester, 78
civitates, 22–4; *12*
Clatchard's Craig, 113
Colchester, 22
Coludesburgh, 92
Columba, St, 52–5, 90–1,
  125; *36, 66*
Congresbury, 117
Constantine III, emperor,
  13–15; *2*
Constantine the Great, em-
  peror, 72
Cormac's *Glossary*, 63
Cornish language, 28–9, 66
Cornwall, 64, 68, 82, 108–
  11, 116
Coroticus, king, 83
Cross-inscribed stones, 108–
  9
Cumbric language, 28
Cunedda, 60, 115

Dalmahoy, 114
Degannwy, 116
Deira, 27
Déisi, 61–2, 66
Denork, 113
Dinas Emrys, 116
Dinas Powys, 116, 135
Dinmelioc, 116
Dinorben, 116
Dumbarton Rock, 115; *93*
Dumium, 70
Dumnonia, 36, 64, 112, 124;
  49, 50
Dumyat, 113
Dunadd, 54, 114; *38*
Dundurn, 113

Dunollie, 54
Dunragit, 115
Dyrham, 69

Eborius, bishop, 78
Edict of Milan, 72
Edwin, king, 98
Elmet, 27
Eochaid Allmuir, 61
Ethelbert, king, 95–6, 98

fields, 122–3; *97*
Finnian, St, 90
foederati(o), 31, 60
Franks, 95–6, 134

Galicia, 70
Galloway, 56
Germanus of Auxerre, St,
  85
Gildas, 21, 33, 61
Glastonbury, 117
Gloucester, 19, 22
Gododdin, 82, 115
Gododdin (poem), 40–1
Gratian, emperor, 15
Gregory the Great, Pope, 95
Guriat, 58–9
Gwithian, 21, 121–3; *97*

Hadrian's Wall, 15, 83; *5, 21*
hand-mill, 119–21; *96*
hanging-bowls, 130; *108*
Hengist and Horsa, 32–3
High Peak, 117
hill forts, 112–17; *22, 92–5*
Hinton St Mary, 74; *55*
Honorius, emperor, 13–15
horses, 124–5

illuminated   manuscripts,
  104–5; *36, 57, 63, 73,
  79–81, 104*
Iona, 55, 65, 92, 99, 102, 125
Irish language, 29

Jarrow, 92, 104
jewellery, 127–34; *99–101,
106, 107*
Julian, martyr, 72
Jutes, 33

keeill, 58
Kentigern, St, 82
Kildare, 124

laeti, 31
Lagore, 135
Lantwit Major, 88
Lérins, 85
Ligugé, 85
Lincoln, 22, 78
Lindisfarne (Holy Isle), 91,
102; *74*
Llandaff, 90
Llyn, 59
London, 19, 22, 78, 96–8
Lullingstone, 74; *53, 54*

Magnus Maximus, emperor,
15, 26, 62; *3*
Mailoc, bishop, 70
Manx language, 30, 58
Marmoutier, 85
Marseilles, 85
Martin of Tours, St, 79, 85
Maughold, 91
meid(i)r, (*moydir*), 57, 60, 66
mercenaries, 134–5
metalwork, 126–34; *102,
103, 105*
monasteries, 84–94; *37, 88*
Monkwearmouth, 92, 104
Mons Badonicus, 39–43
Mote of Mark, 115
Mungo, St, 82
myghtern, 27

Nantcarban, 90
Nennius, 39–40, 98

Ninian, St, 78–85; *35, 58,
59, 101*
Northumbria, 91, 98–103,
111

Offa's Dyke, 36; *19*
ogam, 62–4, 106–7; *47, 85,
86*
Old Melrose, 82, 92
Orkney and Shetland, 91
Oswald, king, 91, 99
Oswin, king, 125

pagus, 26
Palladius, 83
paruchia, 84
Patrick, St, 25, 53, 62, 83–4
Paulinus, 98
Pecthelm, bishop, 79
pecunia, 124
Picts, 16, 27, 30, 33, 42–53,
80, 108, 113, 124
Pictish art, 49–51, 105, 125,
130; *28–32, 98, 108*
Pictish language, 30
ploughs, 121–3; *97*
Potitus, 25
pottery: 'Gwithian style',
65–9
  grass-marked, 56–65; *41*
  imported Mediterranean,
86–8, 116–17; *60, 61*
séricitique, 69
  souterrain ware, 54–6, 65;
40
Powys, 27

Restitutus, bishop, 78
Rheged, 82, 115
Riothamus, king, 68
river-names, 37–8; *20*
rix, 25
Rochester, 98
rotary querns, 119–20
Ruin, The (poem), 36

St Albans, 19–20; *9*
Saxon Shore, 16–18; *6–8*
Sceilg Mhichíl, 94–5; *69, 70*
Scot (t)i, 53, 114
Scottish Gaelic language, 30
scramasax, 134
Silchester, 19
sliabh, 56–7
souterrains, 44; *25–7*
South Cadbury, 117
spatha, 134
spears, 131, 134
'sub-Roman', 19
swords, 134–5

Theodosius, emperor, 15
tigernos, 25
tigos, 119
Tintagel, 88, 189; *62*
Traprain Law, 115; *94*
Tristan, 41–2
Trusty's Hill, 116
tuath, 84

Ui Liathain, 62–4

Valentia, 15, 81
vallum, 92
Vespasian's Camp, 117
Vortigern, 32–3
Votadini, 60, 115
Voteporix, 61

Wales, 82–3, 106, 108–11,
116, 135
Welsh language, 28–9
Whitby, 92, 102
Whithorn, 79–82
Winchester, 19, 24; *75*
Wirral, 58
wolves, 125
Wroxeter, 19

Yeavering, 98
York, 19, 22, 78, 96–8; *71*